SH!TTY GRiT

SH!TTY GRIT

CLAIRE PARKINSON

First published 2025
Copyright © Claire Parkinson 2025

Disclaimer
This story is mostly true. Please note that memory is
inherently subjective, and some details may have been
reconstructed or interpreted with the passage of time.
Details may have been changed for narrative purposes.
Any conclusions, inferences, or interpretations you may
form as a reader are solely your own and do not represent the
views, intentions, or conclusions of the author. This memoir
contains references to drugs and violence that may not be
suitable for younger readers. Discretion is advised.

Typeset by BookPOD

ISBN: 978-1-7638983-0-1 (paperback)
eISBN: 978-1-7638983-1-8 (e-book)

NATIONAL LIBRARY OF AUSTRALIA

A catalogue record for this
book is available from the
National Library of Australia

For little Claire, who hides inside of me.
It is OK to come out now.
Your light will never be dimmed.

Contents

1

Confessions of a Jailbird

How the hell did I end up here, standing at the gates of a prison like I was about to audition for an adults-only version of Survivor: The Penis Edition?

'Oh shit!' I muttered, little realising at that moment that 'shit' was destined to play a leading role in my life – both figuratively and literally.

It was just after 6:50 am, and I marched confidently to my first-ever responsible job, feeling like a rookie superhero about to save the day at one of Her Majesty's finest facilities.

I smiled from ear to ear as I crossed the icy wasteland that wintry English morning, my trusty Doc Martens shattering the frozen blades of grass underfoot. As I reached the area that I would later come to know as the Green Mile, a steamy fog billowed from my mouth with every exhaled breath. The crunching of my boots felt loud enough to wake the sleeping beauties within the foreboding walls.

As I vainly attempted to lower each foot and step forward without making a sound, my thoughts drifted off to a youth spent on a nondescript English council estate. Pregnant at sixteen, I had nowhere to call home and had been thrown onto a merry-go-round of wank jobs, poor-life choices, and dysfunctional relationships.

I could almost hear the condescending howls of derision from the many in my life who assured me that if luck didn't just happen to come my way, I would end up a benefits baroness, wearing ankle-high, nude-coloured UGG boots – not the fancy designer ones – and saggy tracksuit pants, as I made my way through a life of shabbiness and long dole queues.

Family and friends delighted in telling me that unless a rich older man stepped in to take control of my life, prison would surely await me. My army of naysayers had got that one right. Prison did indeed await me, only it was I who held the keys.

I felt good about a career choice that I had hoped would be filled with adventure. I realise now how pivotal that decision was and how it saw me rise from clown cadet prison officer to a governor in some of the UK's toughest prisons.

My eyes inadvertently surveyed my uniform that practically screamed 'I'm important', and my black men's size 32 trousers, cut so low they could have been a fashion statement for rebellious teens. Then there was the long stave – or truncheon, for those not in the know – hiding in the pocket behind the left knee. That thing was only ever used once, and it was not a glamorous moment. I was sprinting down a staircase like a frenzied gazelle in response to the incident alarm bell, when my trusty truncheon wedged itself behind my knee, acting much like pushing a stick into the spokes of a bike. I performed a spectacular cartwheel to the base of the stairwell in what I can only describe as a near-death experience. Yep, the new clown was in town, there for the inmates' entertainment.

The outline of the prison building emerging through the early morning misty gloom refocused my mind on the day ahead. It was a massive double-storey brick structure, with formidable double metal gates at the entrance that opened onto a small porch. There, a solid double wooden door led to the central staff administration office, known colloquially as the Bubble, behind which was another set of large and sturdy gates that led towards the cell blocks. Once the gates slammed shut, the Bubble was a quarantined, prisoner free zone.

The cell blocks had magnolia walls and each cell had a blue door. The cells ran the full length of the two identical wings fanning out in opposite directions. Each wing had an upstairs and downstairs landing, and both were equipped with two communal ablution facilities. In many ways, it was a contemporary prison with ample light, numerous roof vents for smoke extraction should a fire break out, and a grassed football pitch in the foreground. Any notion of it being a college campus was quickly dispelled by the almost seventeen-foot fencing encircling it. However, at a glance, one might mistake the 'students' inside the perimeter fence for aspiring taxidermists. Media reports revealed dead pigeons, their stomachs stuffed with drugs, were strategically tossed over the fence, turning them into prized hunting trophies.

As the lone female on a team tasked with caring for hundreds of mischievous, presumably sex-starved inmates at this Suffolk prison, I was fortunate that I had already gained plenty of skills and experience when it came to handling men. This had certainly not always been the case. In my younger days, I believed men were my golden ticket to happiness, where my rich future husband would allow me to enjoy all the trappings of luxury, if not love.

Shallow as a puddle and drowning in naivety, I spun my own fairy-tale stories. They became my reality, embodying everything I believed my life had been lacking. I was grateful those days were behind me, and I avoided asking Dr Google what psychological disorder had driven my desperate need for attention from strangers.

However, my knack for handling men transferred seamlessly to the prison environment, helping me persuade the lads to clean the unit and polish the floors, turning their chores into something fun on an otherwise boring-as-bat-shit day. The wing sparkled with a fresh, healthy sheen.

But I soon learnt boys will forever be boys. One particularly chilly, minus-whatever-it-was morning, I crossed the icy wasteland to the cell blocks to wake the prisoners. It was nudging 7:00 am, and I was the first on the cell block ready to perform the morning roll call of the day shift. My job was straightforward. I would lift each cell flap to expose a glass viewing window, shine a torch in and count two prisoners in each cell. With one on the top bunk and the other on the bottom, I would tick them off as present and still alive. The first cell flap squeaked open as my powerful torch beam pierced the darkness, scanning the bleak surroundings before settling on the cold steel framework of the top bunk. It was clear that the fellow up there was having what I can politely describe as 'a moment' with himself. Unfazed, I continued to the next cell, determined to count the two hundred or so men as quickly as possible and get on with the day's other tasks. Again, the top bunk inhabitant was wrestling with his one-eyed snake. This scene was repeated across the next few cells before, with frozen hands and tortured eyes, I realised I had been part of a prisoner conspiracy to show the new screw some cock. They had expected me to reel in horror, get all flustered and scuttle off to tell my male boss – but they had picked on the wrong girl.

I said nothing as I headed back to the Bubble, hung up my coat, and took a deep breath. Then, with a small smile, I reached out and flicked the switch that lit up the building like a Christmas tree. My small smile turned into one of a Cheshire Cat as I turned the office radio to its usual mind-numbing channel. Taking great care, I taped down the tannoy loudspeaker button to ensure that the entire wing got a dose of its flaccid penis playlist. 'That should flop the mop,' I mumbled quietly.

The reaction was immediate. A cacophony of moans filled the cell block as doors were kicked and grumblings floated down the wings, all suggesting that at least some degree of restorative justice had been served. I calmly pulled the microphone closer and gave it an obligatory tap.

'Morning boys, it's your favourite female officer here and I just want to reassure you all that I have noted your need for a magnifying glass and the purchase order has been raised,' I announced in my most officious voice.

A round of applause erupted around the unit. It felt good to hold my own. I had stood my ground, sending a clear message that I wasn't a pushover, nor an arsehole who couldn't take a joke. Technically, I should have followed the formal disciplinary procedure for bad prisoner behaviour and issued them all a report card. But as a mother to a son,

I knew the best way to handle their antics wasn't through punitive paperwork. Instead, I turned their joke around, earned their respect, and let laughter work its magic. For the first time since joining the Prison Service, an emotion of empowerment replaced the insecurities that had clung to me since graduating from Prison College.

My thoughts darted back to my first probationary year, during which every happy-go-lucky breath had been sucked out of me.

My first posting as a full-time prison officer took me to the segregation unit of a women's prison around an hour from my home in Haverhill, a dormitory town some fifty miles northeast of London. Prisoners are held in segregation for a variety of reasons, but generally, it boils down to two main factors: either they are unable to function among the mostly decent but flawed individuals in the normal wings, or they require protection because their crimes are so heinous they risk revenge attacks by fellow inmates.

I was a bouncy twenty-something recruit, unaccustomed to dealing with such a stifling environment. I was different in many ways – young, raw, and carrying a risky and jovial disposition. It was obvious to me that I raised eyebrows, with some probably branding me a dick. I cried a lot in those early days, questioning why the carefree fairy-tale world I had long believed in wasn't panning out according to script.

It's a little embarrassing to admit that I was tipped over the edge the day I arrived to find doughnuts had been bought for morning tea. My tummy grumbled while impatiently waiting for the tea break. When I joined the tearoom table, everyone was munching on their fried bit of confectionery and the container was empty. While I knew it wasn't intentional, the dearth of doughnuts brought tears to my eyes. But I instinctively knew I could survive going without a doughnut. I had already confronted teenage motherhood and faced up to the painful realisation that in the real world, the boy-meets-girl-and-they-live-happily-ever-after fairy tale is largely bollocks.

Slumped in the prison tearoom, engulfed in self-pity, I was filled with dread that I might end up through some weird process of osmosis, a grown-up – working nine to five, hating my job, tired all the time, whinging about my spouse, and rambling on about the weather.

On my first day as an active prison officer, I met the notorious Myra Hindley and spent the next twelve months as one of her personal officers. I often accompanied her on her daily hour of fresh air when she traded her cell for the exercise yard.

The yard was a secure space measuring around twenty feet by fifteen feet, surrounded by an internal fence that blocked any view in or out. Dark, dank, and depressing, it featured little more than a patch of lawn in the centre and a single paved path that ran along the perimeter.

Myra, along with her boyfriend Ian Brady, was an infamous serial killer jailed for life for the so-called Moors Murders of five children in the UK. Online records indicate that the horrific rampage took place between July 1963 and October 1965. This meant most UK adults at that time knew of the Moors Murders, and very few crimes generated such public loathing.

It is said that Myra fell madly in love with Brady to the point where she was under his spell and willing to surrender to his total control. Their first murder victim was Pauline Reade, who was heading to a local dance just like any other sixteen-year-old. A few months later, twelve-year-old John Kilbride was snatched, sexually assaulted and murdered. The duo's next victim, Keith Bennett, also aged twelve, was snatched on an evening in June 1964, just four days after his birthday. The bespectacled boy was walking to visit his grandmother and was never seen again, and his body has never been found.

On a chilly Boxing Day in 1964, ten-year-old Lesley Ann Downey was lured away from a funfair, abducted, raped and murdered by the pair. Her body was dumped in a shallow grave on Saddleworth Moor and lay undiscovered until October 1965. Brady then went on to bludgeon seventeen-year-old Edward Evans to death.

Myra's younger brother-in-law, David Smith, was also said to be involved in the horrific murder of Evans, but fearing he would succumb to a similarly sadistic end, alerted the police.

Hindley was convicted of killing Lesley Ann, Edward, and John, as well as assisting in the abduction and murder of Keith. She was also convicted of shielding Brady after John's murder and was jailed for life. Some twenty years later, the pair admitted to killing Keith and Pauline, and assisted the police in locating Pauline's remains. However, Brady took the secret of where Keith's remains were located to his own grave in 2017, while he was still serving time at Her Majesty's pleasure.

Myra was in her mid-fifties and had been a prisoner for over thirty years when I entered her world in January 1998. As a lifer, she would never again see the outside world. If there was any hope of her rehabilitation after what she had done, the vehemence of public opinion against her demanded that justice be delivered by her serving every second of the rest of her life in prison and dying behind bars.

Dressed in baggy, prison-appropriate clothing, she shuffled about slowly and purposefully in her slippers. Her head mostly bowed, her nicotine-stained fingers would repeatedly lift a cigarette to a row of similarly discoloured teeth. She was unremarkable but for the fact that she was Myra Hindley, the perpetrator of heinous crimes. She always struck me as being a little reserved, but mild-mannered and polite, which created a conflict of professional versus real-life ethics for me. I was curious to engage with her and try to understand what made this now frail woman tick. While I never befriended Myra, I was able to build a rapport while going about my duties of keeping her occupied and engaged. I spoke with her most days, mainly just general chit-chat rather than anything deep. I was strangely grateful for the conversation, as the segregation unit can be a lonely and isolating place. I was careful never to ask Myra about her crimes, what drove her to commit them or how she felt about Ian Brady all these years later. I often wondered though, if she harboured any regrets, or felt genuinely remorseful for doing the unthinkable. I was tempted to ask her, but knew if I went down that dark alley, I would form an opinion and forever forfeit my non-judgmental position, leading me to treat her differently.

During Myra's sixty minutes of her version of freedom in the exercise yard each day, she, like just about every other prisoner in the world, would walk anticlockwise. With each slow and deliberate footstep she took, I would watch, marginally spellbound as I tried to glean something from her gait and facial expressions. I wondered what her nightmares consisted of and how she coped with the isolation. Then the alarm would sound to signal her time was up and Groundhog Day began again.

It was courteous practice for another officer to take over exercise yard duty once a prisoner had completed their one-hour outing and was escorted back to the isolation of their cell. However, I was happy to stay out in the yard as I oddly enjoyed spending hours outside in the cold and damp chatting to prisoners. The only downside, as I saw it, was that I'd step out with my shiny, straightened hair, only to come back looking as though I'd dropped my hairdryer into the bath, with me in it, resulting in a startling resemblance to Leo Sayer.

While working with someone incarcerated can give you deep insight into the world of an institutionalised person, successful prison staff know not to cross the line and befriend prisoners. Those that do, often have their disasters – usually of the sexual nature – splashed across the pages of *The Sun*. In hindsight, staff members who tended to get it wrong were easy to spot – the plain, middle-aged man or woman, who had access to prisoners and seemed to lack confidence, perhaps even feeling a little inadequate in the real world. Probably, for the first time in a long time, they received attention from an admirer. They would fail to appreciate that the interest was coming from a prisoner who was so desperate for something to break the monotony of their prison time, that he or she had long since farewelled being fussy. That prisoner would likely seek extra cash from the misguided staff member, to spend on the limited selection of goodies in the prison shop, or sometimes, the relationship would progress to them smuggling illegal substances into the prison for the prisoner, with their misguided service being repaid in sexual favours. Good old-fashioned love rarely entered the equation in these relationships.

During my first year working with the women prisoners, I often felt like I didn't belong in the Prison Service. Dealing with high-maintenance prisoners who would happily throw shit pots, hurl abuse and even bite and spit at me was far from enjoyable.

One eventful day, prisoner Suzie had decided the best way to end her life was by tying her G-string knickers around her throat after swallowing a used sanitary towel. Clearly, she wasn't firing on all cylinders and on this day, she was on my watch. I wrestled with this troubled young woman to clear her airways and managed to pull the 'unsanitary' item from her mouth. However, Suzie snatched it from my hand and stuck it firmly to my forehead. Had it not been so disgusting, I would probably have found it funny, especially as it reminded me of my childhood days when playing hospital wards with my girlfriends. We would innocently stick our mothers' panty-liners to our foreheads and paint a little red cross in the middle to identify us as nurses.

As the junior screw, I had a lot to learn, as evidenced by an event a few days later. While delivering the midday meal to the cells, a confident young four-foot-nothing wisp of a prisoner named Monica asked me what fish was on the menu. I didn't have a clue, which ignited the smart-arse in me.

'It's a fish, with a tail and gills,' I told her.

Her cold stare cut through me like a scalpel as I closed her door and moved on to deliver lunch to the next cell. I thought little of it as the afternoon wore on and I attended to the duties that make up a prison officer's day. My reminder came later when opening Monica's cell ahead of her daily exercise outing. She had obviously been stewing since lunch, along with her half-full pot of shit and piss, which she offloaded on my head, its fetid contents rolling down my uniform. I probably deserved what I got and quickly learnt that it was not wise to get lippy with people who had lost their liberty and had lots of thinking time on their hands.

Looking back on that chaotic first year in prison, I realised I had somehow emerged as a reluctant expert in the art of survival – albeit with a used sanitary towel still haunting my forehead like a ghastly badge of honour. I'd navigated the challenges of high-maintenance prisoners and learnt how to dodge flying faeces. Strangely, I felt almost grateful for the hard lessons. In the prisoners I cared for, I saw aspects of myself – particularly my flippancy. Like me, they wielded humour as a shield, using it to deflect the harshness of their surroundings.

My experiences, courtesy of Her Majesty's Prison, were reshaping me in ways I never expected. I began to understand the subtle eyebrow raises from my more experienced colleagues when, on the brink of a crisis, instead of a seasoned officer as their backup, they found themselves with a clueless newbie who tried to make everything into a joke, sometimes at the most inappropriate times.

I might not be a fully-fledged adult yet, but I'd definitely taken the training wheels off. Life wasn't the fairy tale I'd once imagined, but it was the only story I knew how to live. I was beginning to realise that the outcomes of my actions had little to do with luck.

2

Haver–init–all

How is it that a carefree childhood filled with laughter and mischief can collide so spectacularly with adulthood's relentless quest for acceptance?

My story kicks off in Haverhill, a nondescript settlement in Suffolk. It's just seventeen miles from Cambridge, but in every other way, it felt light-years away from the prestigious university town the rest of the world admired.

Ours was a standard working-class family, occupying a modest council house nestled in one of the many government-owned housing estates flanking the town. Dating back to at least the Saxon times, Haverhill is proudly recorded in the Domesday Book of 1086. Its better-known modern history began in the 1950s, when it was significantly expanded to house communities relocated from London after World War II. New housing estates quickly sprang up along with numerous factories to provide homes and employment for the growing population. From the early 1960s to my teenage years in the mid-1980s, the population swelled from around five thousand to nearly twenty-five thousand.

Our family consisted of Mum, Dad, my older brother and me. I was a slim girl, tall for my age, with huge feet, which resulted in my parents nicknaming me Freddo Frog.

Dad was a long-distance lorry driver whose job delivering coal to various parts of the country would keep him away all week. Mum did a few hours a week in cleaning jobs, and my brother could best be described as a sibling okay enough to tolerate but giving me many moments wishing I was an only child.

Dad had a wicked sense of humour and a knack for telling captivating stories. He was a man with a powerful presence, who, when needed, could turn us into trembling, over-obedient kids in the mould of the Von Trapp family.

Late each Friday afternoon, the instantly recognisable hiss of his lorry suspension as he rounded the final corner would signal his return home. As kids, it was music to our ears and as the apple of Daddy's eye, I would always run out to greet him.

Dad had his set routine, which we called wind-down hour. It started in the kitchen, where he'd empty his lunch bag and meticulously scrub every plate, bowl, drinking mug, and cooking utensil. Each item would be dried with the care of a man preparing a Michelin-star meal, before being carefully packed into his travel bag for the week ahead. Then in complete silence, he'd make his slow, deliberate trek up the stairs to the bathroom for a long, luxuriating bath. It was as though he was summoning the soap and water to drag him back to the real world. We knew not to disturb him until the ritual was complete. When he emerged, he was the fun Dad we adored, and he would regale us with stories of his week. Seated around the dinner table we were captivated and in varying fits of laughter as he recounted stories about life on the road. He was brilliant at describing every minute detail and had an ability to paint a vivid story. There were even tales of the ladies of the night who would approach the parked trucks, knock on their doors, and ask the dozing truckies if they might be interested in a little company within the confines of their cab.

Dad taught me to accept other people's life choices, and to laugh at myself, even when tears might seem more appropriate. I admired him deeply.

Mum's role was as the family's anchor and her quiet strength held everything together while he was away. Mum worked tirelessly to keep the family going, maintaining a sense of order in the house and making sure we were all properly fed.

Mum's early life was incredibly tough. She lost her mother to tuberculosis when she was just a baby and was later raised by her grandmother after her father remarried. Struggling with tuberculosis for much of her childhood meant she spent many years in isolation, which understandably shaped her into a more reserved person as an adult. Despite these challenges, Mum's strength and resilience were always evident in everything she did for our family.

My brother was in many ways my opposite – quiet, academically minded and considered. Standing over six feet tall by the age of thirteen, with short, curly, blond hair and a face that was the scene of a freckles and acne battlefield, he was certainly not a chiselled model. But he always seemed to be in the company of young women queuing for his attention. He didn't follow fashion, choosing to live in shorts and T-shirts as he pursued his passion for sport, with football being his favourite. Being four years my senior, he treated me as the little sister who was too young to partake in his interests. The distance between us was further exacerbated by a UK educational system where we were never in the same school. He had long since moved to middle school when I entered primary school, and by the time I had made my way to middle school, he had graduated to high school. This meant he was way cooler than me and hanging out with a younger sister was his quickest path to 'coolness lost'.

I committed myself to being a royal pain in his arse. I moaned incessantly about his bedroom being larger than mine and demanded equality from my parents. In the end, my persistent whining drove them to splash out their limited funds to demolish the wall between our rooms and create two equally sized spaces.

Our home was certainly not flash, but it was safe and comforting. The entrance hall had a small toilet off to the left, with the dining room and adjoining kitchen ahead. A comfortable sitting room completed the cosy, heated, downstairs area. The temperature then plummeted with each step going upstairs to the three bedrooms, another toilet and the family bathroom. There was plush carpeting but this couldn't compensate for the absence of upstairs heating, making it arctic for most of the year.

The fashion of the era insisted that every wall of a home was covered in wallpaper. The most memorable decor was in the sitting room, where the walls were covered in an artistic array of repetitive bamboo with interwoven flowers that were the backdrop to our mint-green velvet sofa. Unfortunately, my parents chose to disrupt this creative serenity with a beige floral carpet.

It was normal in the UK during the 1980s for families to be on the large side with enough kids to make a football team. Our unit of a part-time working Mum, a full-time working Dad and two children, made us somewhat different to the point where some in the community considered us posh. So, I soon understood that even in the world of the working-class and council housing, there is a pecking order, determined by whether or not you have an income.

Our 'posh' status heightened when Dad decided to replace the lower exterior wooden façade with brick. Black tarpaulin was draped from ceiling to floor while Dad went about this renovation project. Months later when he unveiled the completed masterpiece, our council estate friends were quick to give it the nickname of 'the Castle' and brand us the snobs who lived behind its walls. I wanted nothing more than to fit in, and despite not knowing what posh or snob really meant, I was smart enough to know that it wasn't a desirable tag on a council estate.

As my teen years approached, I began to develop a competitive eye for boys. Flat-chested when compared with my friends and although not the front-running beauty, I was well-appreciated by the young males in the neighbourhood. A new-found brash confidence defied my previously coy exterior and a growing collection of swear words entered my vocabulary.

My friends were all a bit feral, but we were good kids. We weren't interested in fashion, and boys held little appeal, that is, until Dave waltzed into our lives. He would obligingly meet us girls at the grandiosely named

Love Mountain, a hillock of household garden waste that had hardened and become covered in weeds and a few blades of lush green grass. We would patiently await our turn for kissing lessons from our new teacher Dave, queuing with watchful longing and anticipation as those before us moved into position to kiss this obliging guy. Dave was aloofness personified, caring little about who he kissed. In contrast, we girls were in total awe and fawning all over him with eyes and mouths wide open. I would stand in line and count in my head how long each Dave-pashing session took, determined to ensure that when my turn came, I got more kissing time than any of the others. Finally, our lips touched, and the intoxicating exchange of saliva dared our darting tongues to intertwine. Despite breathing becoming difficult, my competitive streak took over and I held on as I needed to kiss him for longer than anyone else to be the best kisser. I had to stand alone as the kissing queen of Haverhill.

Our fun was mostly harmless but I'm sure it was annoying for the locals. We would play in the fields around the estate, climb oak trees, scrump apples by scaling neighbours' fences, and knock loudly on people's doors before running off and hiding. We would collect shopping trolleys from the local shops and place them strategically over raw sewage silos then leapfrog over them. It was fun with a splash of smelly risk and always had us squealing with laughter.

Nothing came close to amusing us quite like the whoopee cushion game that we reserved for the bona fide posh folk of Haverhill. They lived in the large bungalows set back from the street with manicured lawns neatly dissected by a long concrete pathway. As the mischief leader for our group, I took the daring role of marching up to their homes with my friends in tow. I would knock on their front doors as they peered out from behind their fashionable white net curtains. My juvenile hands clutching my fanny while I twisted my legs like ancient grapevines, I would deliver an Oscar-winning performance of someone about to wet themselves and feverishly pleaded to use their bathroom. Once inside, I would haul out the whoopee cushion from under my jumper, slowly inflate it with a long, silent blow, then place it on the toilet seat. I'd lower myself onto it and twist and turn to emit a barrage of farts until my friends' laughter filled the hallway. We thought we were geniuses for devising such hilarity. We were sure these kind folk who let us use their bathrooms had no idea we were tricking them. The wonderful naivety bubble was soon burst when one of the cunning posh homeowners called the law and I was afforded the privilege of my first ride home in a police car.

Anchored in a world of toilet humour, our political education was rudimentary. The only names I knew were Margaret Thatcher and Arthur Scargill. She was the Iron Lady, the I'm-going-to-kick-your-arse politician, and he was the manly chest-beating respondent. Our fuzzy black-and-white fourteen-inch telly showed him with an army of strident workers in the background, chanting slogans and cheering his every word. But I was more drawn to Margaret Thatcher, not because of her political alignment or her views, but because as a woman she was fearless, with an abundance of grit. I respected her and wanted to be known as fearless and tough too, but with the added bonus of being hot! My first attempt at blending these three ideals was when I met the next person to fundamentally shape me.

Timmy was one of those boys all the girls fancied. Entering masculinity before most of his classmates, he was the epitome of tall, dark, and handsome. He didn't attend the same school as me, which made him mysterious and fresh blood as well. My stomach filled with a kaleidoscope of butterflies as I caught my first glimpse of him across a crowded community hall disco. At the tender age of eleven, the sight of him whetted my courage. As the DJ placed a slow record on the turntable, I stood up, stuck out my yet-to-develop chest, and strode over. He nodded a distinctive yes to my wanton invitation to dance, and in a vice-like grip, we smooched for an eternity like pink flamingoes during mating season. My crush had developed into love by the end of the second song.

Timmy and I would see each other at various discos and as with Dave on Love Mountain, he was an irresistible lady magnet and in high demand. I reluctantly accepted that I would need to bide my time behind the harem of contemporaries equally impressed by this fine specimen. My elation knew no bounds when Timmy eventually asked me to accompany him to a party. We were going to be boyfriend and girlfriend and live happily ever after.

Struggling to contain my excitement, I spent hours fidgeting and getting ready that Saturday, all the while dreaming of Timmy collecting me and us galloping off into the sunset together, stopping only to gaze adoringly into each another's eyes. I watched the hall clock and counted down the minutes to the agreed collection time of six o'clock. The emptiness I felt when the anticipated ring of the doorbell failed to materialise was horrific. I waited and watched the minutes on the clock tick by while repeatedly playing Dad's *Carpenters Gold* LP record. The clock struck seven o'clock, and there was still no Timmy. My devastation had Dad turning red with rage at witnessing his little girl's heart being broken for the first time. Without uttering a word, he grabbed his jacket from behind the front door and disappeared into the night.

Dad returned about an hour later to announce that he had visited Timmy's house to inform his mother that her dastardly son had wronged his princess. Timmy's mum was an instant ally and marched over to the party to locate a snogging Timmy and unhinge him from whomever he had become attached. She then dragged him out of the party and frog-marched him home. Timmy was grounded, and in a single, traumatic moment, our happily-ever-after bliss vanished. Dad had scared the shit out of him. He wasn't coming back, and my heart was totally broken.

At some point, my carefree, mischievous childhood tilted on its axis into a frantic race for approval. It was at that moment I realised life didn't come with a foolproof adulting manual.

3

Semen or Amniotic fluid...

Until this occasion, I'd always believed my parents had the answer to everything. But on this day, they were so out of their depth, they didn't know whether to call a priest, a therapist, or a hitman. There I was, being wheeled away like some poor soul on a peculiar episode of The Price is Right, where instead of a new car, the grand prize was a lifetime subscription to pure fuckwittery.

Every girl knows the antidote to being stood up is retail therapy, and at eleven years old, I was already a connoisseur of its healing powers. I begged Mum for a hamster to replace Timmy – mainly because they're adorable and less likely to stand me up. But, while I thought Mum was out of touch, she had her wits about her and quickly shot down my request. Undeterred, I decided to defy her – after all, who could resist the charm of a fluffy little rodent?

My window shopping at the local pet shop soon had me ditch the hamster idea – largely because there weren't any in stock. So, in my rush to mend my bleeding heart, I bought a beautiful white mouse with a long pink tail and headed home. I was surprised that Mum didn't share my rodent love. I was even more surprised when she chased me up the stairs while slapping the back of my legs twenty-two times, and simultaneously yelling, 'How. Dare. You. Disobey. Me. You. Can. Keep. That. Fucking. Mouse. In. Your. Bedroom. And. See. How. Much. You. Like. The. Smell!'

'He's not a fucking mouse,' I shouted back, 'he's family and he's called Timmy.'

'More like a rat then!' she retorted.

Timmy did as Mum had predicted, and as my little room became engulfed in a cocktail of ammonia mouse smells, I did the smart thing and returned him to the pet shop. A mouse just wasn't going to cut it. I needed a boyfriend.

School strikes were in progress across the UK. Teachers were marching with slogans for more pay daubed on sandwich boards. Rolling school closures were the norm. My school wasn't on strike that fateful day, and as I left the grounds, there he was, sitting astride his shining new silver-coloured Diamond Back BMX. My Timmy replacement had arrived.

I hadn't met Max before, although stories about him were legendary. A recent arrival from London, he was said to be the coolest kid Haverhill had ever seen. I had to agree, even though I had no benchmark against which to measure him, as he was the first lifelong-Londoner I had met. His trendy light grey, almost-blue Lois cords with base splits sat nicely over his phenomenal Nike Airs. His lemon-yellow designer Kappa T-shirt perfectly complemented the outfit. He oozed poise and style, even if his head was a bit big – in the literal, rather than metaphorical sense. Actually, it wasn't just big, it was fucking humongous. It had enjoyed a growth spurt all on its own, reaching adulthood while the rest of his body was stuck in puberty and had clearly not received the growth memo. He was quite a sight – funny-looking, if I'm brutally honest – but we were kids, and funny was fine with me. He looked every bit a member of the London set, who were not only exposed to fancy branded attire but had the taste, the means, and the attitude to pull it off. How could a girl's heart not melt amid all that coolness, especially after Timmy's cold shoulder? Max *had* to be my boyfriend!

Max came from a family considerably wealthier than ours, with his parents presumed to have a mortgage on a pleasant home that had never been a council house. He always had a stash of cash in his pocket, which was not something I'd experienced before. Our friendship started slowly, progressing to the point where he made a habit of being outside my school every afternoon, and we'd catch up with a bit of flirting. I could tell I was making progress, weaving my way into his heart, and I let myself imagine a future with Max – a future that seemed big, bright, and full of possibilities. Then, one world-ending day, he wasn't at the school gates to meet me. The he-doesn't-like-me-anymore thought was almost unbearable. As I walked home, tears streaming down my face from the rejection, I heard a familiar voice call out from a distance, 'Oi, scab!'

I knew what 'scab' meant, as I had seen Mr Scargill and his supporters waving placards condemning those who chose to work while a strike was on. I knew it wasn't nice, but that didn't matter, because Max's school was on strike and mine wasn't, so I wasn't a scab, and I wasn't crossing any picket lines. So, all I heard was a symphony of love notes flying from his lips and wafting over towards me. I turned to see him toss something in my direction. As it tumbled through the air, I recognised it as his precious gold Saint Christopher necklace. I jumped forward to catch it, heard strains of *Chariots of Fire*, and fixed my eyes on him. He looked back at me for what felt like an eternity, before delivering a laid-back nod of the head and riding off. It was hardly the stuff of Jane Austen, but as I placed the Saint Christopher around my neck and felt the coolness of the yellow metal on my skin for the first time, I instantly knew its significance. I was now his girlfriend, and I would soon officially become Mrs Max.

As we clumsily plodded into puberty, sex became an all-consuming topic for me and my friends. We talked about it daily, and some even shared the momentous news that they had 'done it'. With each new revelation, my virginity hung heavily over me like the sword of Damocles.

Two weeks into my budding romance with Max, my best friend lost her virginity to a boy named Steven – envy and impatience got the better of me. I asked her to arrange for him to assist me in losing this virginal burden in my life. Steven the Stud had olive skin and dark, wavy hair. He was not a typical pretty boy and deviated somewhat from the type I was usually attracted to. But he did have a rugged sexiness that made him perfect for breeding in a wild-animal kind of way. He also had a reputation as a lady's man, which grew more powerful every time he was spotted kissing some of the cooler girls around town. Being a school year his junior, I certainly wasn't in the cool-girl category in his eyes. Regardless, he turned out to be the obliging sort and kindly accomplished the task while we walked his dog in a field at the back of his home.

The whole experience was underwhelming at best. I am sure it happened, although, in the absence of a witness I could have been mistaken. Without a hint of foreplay, he swiftly navigated his periscope into position. He didn't even bother to let go of his dog as he got to work in the missionary position. With his face firmly planted in the grass above my right shoulder, there was no romance, no kissing, and the only sound was his dog panting. He pumped a few times, and it was over almost as quickly as it had started. He stood up, zipped his jeans, and said he was going indoors to watch football on the television. I wasn't sure if I was supposed to thank him or whether he would thank me, and before the silence became painful, I spluttered, 'Cheers, Steven,' as I got to my feet and pulled up my pants.

He gave me a look that suggested he thought I was weird. We quickly walked to the side gate that would take us back onto the path home then I went one way, and he went the other.

It was all new to me, and I had no lasting memory of the event. To be honest, I would have preferred a slow dance with a Metallica head-spin kiss. I was not smart enough to realise losing one's virginity was something to behold. To me, it was all about ticking boxes and I had ticked the 'no longer a virgin' box. I was now that little bit cooler and sexually equal to Max. Neither of us would be virgins when we finally sealed the deal – surely Max couldn't be a virgin? I didn't think to ask...

Max and I meandered through our self-absorbed teenage lives. Both sixteen, we would regularly bunk school and have sex, mostly at my house when my parents were out. We'd also kill time at his parents' pub after hours, sneaking downstairs to help ourselves to booze. Holding hands, eating greasy Chinese takeaways and having sex, our relationship was a juvenile, carefree love with the alcohol only adding to what I considered perfection.

I'd been clever enough to introduce another little grown-up chemical into my life after a trip to the family planning clinic. The contraceptive pill now made me the ruler of my sexual health – officially stepping into the world of responsible adulthood. In reality, I was still waist-deep in immaturity and was rarely disciplined enough to take my birth control pill each day. My casual attitude towards this tiny pharmaceutical marvel inevitably caught up with me...

On that fateful day, we found ourselves having a passionate grope session, not in a bed with fine linen, but on a rusty disused railway track. In a show of chivalry that rivalled Sir Walter Raleigh, Max removed his orange puffer jacket to create a bed. While the experience was like my earlier virginity-losing moment, with Max hopping on and off like he was riding a London bus, there was a significant difference. I liked Max and I knew he was my happy ever after. That night, lying on the disused railway track, he told me he loved me, and I believed him. Lying back in the afterglow, I looked up at the night sky and told my love I could see six twinkling stars, which probably meant we would go on to marry and have six children.

'What fucking maths set are you in?' he asked, as we both looked back up at a sky that danced with millions of stars. We rolled around, laughing at the thought of what our future family might look like if the stars meant anything.

The months passed – Max had finished his schooling and had started an apprenticeship as a plumber, or was it a welder? I can't remember, such was my deep interest in his career... My sole focus was my happy ever after with him. My boredom with school increased and I sat my 'O' level exams without giving a toss about the outcome.

I started to look increasingly pasty, with dark circles under my eyes. I also felt under the weather and took it to be the onset of the flu. Cursing this lingering bug for a few weeks and reassuring myself that the medical profession would fix me, I made an appointment with our family doctor.

He was a pleasant young fellow with a beguiling smile. After a few leading questions, he motioned towards the examination table and tapped it.

'Right, young lady, up here,' he said. 'Let's have a little feel of your stomach.'

He had barely touched my tummy when he turned to skinny bean me and said the three words I was hopelessly ill-equipped to hear.

'You are pregnant.'

'That's impossible,' I shot back with all the piety of the Virgin Mary.

His you-are-a-total-wanker look straight into my eyes told me he didn't buy the Immaculate Conception line I was about to peddle. He quietly suggested that I come back later that day for a scan, as he felt the pregnancy was advanced.

Strangely, I didn't leave the surgery in a daze of angst. I was so immature I didn't understand the enormity of my situation. I had no appreciation of what it meant for my now and for my future. Afterall, in my world, teenage pregnancy was no big deal, nothing out of the ordinary, and pretty much a rite of passage judging by the number of teens pushing their toddlers around the town.

In an age before mobile phones, I made my way to the nearest red telephone box, yanked a coin from my pocket, and called Max.

'Max, I'm pregnant,' I said.

'Oh, okay. What do you want to do?' he replied.

'Dunno,' I mumbled.

'Okay, but remember, that baby in your tummy is our baby,' he said gently, before suggesting that we should break the news to our mums and hear what they had to say. 'Remember, it's your decision, I love you and that's all that matters,' he assured me.

He had taken the news remarkably well. I stood in the phone booth for a good few minutes, trying to envisage the future. The immediate required us to tell our families; the long term ignited images of a happy and functional family.

Approaching the discussion with my mother would be relatively easy. She was practical and well-controlled, likely the result of her increasing disappointment over most of the teenage choices I had made so far.

As we sat in front of the television that evening, I literally spat it out: 'Mum, I'm pregnant.'

'Oh, that's not a surprise, you silly, silly girl,' my mother replied, while shaking her head and getting up from the sofa to wash the dishes.

Within a few minutes she returned to the sofa still holding her long-armed yellow rubber gloves. 'How the hell am I supposed to tell your dad that news?' she asked rhetorically.

I decided to attend the scan alone, as I felt it was my decision and didn't want anyone there to influence it. My immaturity prevented me from fully understanding the significance of such an event. Walking up the stairs to the GP's surgery, I felt numb and confused about the emotions I was expected to have. I was alone and for the first time in my young life, I was about to make an adult decision with lasting consequences.

My scan confirmed I was almost twenty weeks pregnant. I made my way to the doctor's rooms to discuss my options and waited patiently outside until the green light above his door flickered brightly to indicate that he was ready for me. I rose slowly, took the short steps to the closed door, gave the customary two polite knocks, turned the cold handle, and entered his surgery.

What had started as a casual and somewhat belated visit to the doctor in search of a flu remedy had become a whirlwind day of emotions. In my see-saw state, I didn't know what to think. I wanted someone to step in, take control, and help me make the biggest decision of my life.

'Take a seat,' he said in a deadpan tone. 'If you choose to have an abortion, we will have to dismember the foetus and suck it out, limb by limb, as it is already too large to remove in one piece.'

I didn't need the twelve hours he gave me to come to a decision, as I was instantly horrified at the prospect of cutting up my baby.

That evening, Max, our mothers, and I reconvened. My decision to keep the child surprised both of our mums. While Max's Mum assured us of her unwavering support, my mother's response was simply to stare at the floor and shake her head.

Without looking up, she whispered, 'It is not going to work with a baby in the house.'

I knew in an instant what she meant. Life in the family home was not an option anymore. I had brought shame on the family. I had shattered all hope of walking down the aisle dressed in white.

In that split second, my family home became just my parents' home.

Dad's road trip was nearing its end, and he would be home by the end of the week, signalling my time to vacate. I was still unfazed by my upcoming homeless status as I would be with Max, so wherever it was, it would be perfect.

Mum had felt it unwise to break the news to Dad while he was alone and driving long distances out on the roads of Britain. She also thought it best if someone beyond the family told Dad. I was in no position to share my view, being *persona non-grata* in her eyes at that time. Mum's plan was to book a doctor's appointment for Dad on the spurious grounds that, as we had all had our annual check-ups while he was away, it was his turn.

During the appointment, the family doctor shared the news with Dad alone in the privacy of the surgery on the Friday evening. Mum and I sat at home in an anxious wait for what felt like hours, consumed by thoughts of how Dad would react when he got home. I wrestled with thoughts that he might shout at me or perhaps even disown me. He was my hero; I couldn't bare for that to change.

While I contemplated his reaction, the distinctive sound of approaching footsteps broke the silence. The front door burst open, and my worst fears were realised as soon as I saw his face. He was beyond angry. His face was contorted with disappointment.

I heard the advice my mother had shared with me a few days earlier – it was time to go. I darted through the back door at a pace that put the Diamond Back BMX firmly in second place. I slammed the door and stood on the precipice of my new life.

Spectacularly immature and ill-prepared, I felt excitement rather than fear. A new adventure awaited, away from the discipline of my parents and into a world of freedom. Everything would be okay. I would leave school and get a job. Max and I would find a house, and we would move in together. He loved me and our unborn child, and the three of us would create a wonderful life together.

I headed for the nearest red phone box and called Max. He instantly came to my rescue, and I spent my first night happily in his arms. I didn't give my parents a second thought that night.

The reality of my situation finally began to penetrate my brain after a couple of months of couch surfing at friends' places. When I had overstayed my welcome, I'd sneak home for a few nights here and there, and Max's family's pub was a good fall-back option.

Max's Mum finally stepped in and offered us the rental of one of her investment homes. Being our only chance of a roof over our heads and with me now nearly eight-months pregnant, we jumped at the opportunity to move in together.

Our first home was a small two-up, two-down in a quiet village around the corner from Max's Mum's pub and eight miles from my parents' home. Our happy-ever-after life could now get properly started.

Our little family unit could enjoy life in a cosy end-of-terrace cottage. Inside, everything was small but functional – an entrance hall leading to the lounge, with a kitchen and bathroom at the rear. A spiral wooden staircase led to two upstairs bedrooms, ours and a nursery lovingly prepared for the eagerly anticipated new arrival.

I had managed to secure a job between the chaos of discovering

I was pregnant and leaving school. I was a clerk in the payroll office at a local furniture manufacturing business. As I saw it, it was a full-time inconvenience, but it was well paid at eighty pounds a week.

At work, I was required to use my head and put my math skills to use. Walking through the factory was often accompanied by wolf whistles, which added an ego boost to the role as I enjoyed the attention, playfully tossing my hair back and forth as I went. With Max's apprentice wage, we had enough money to survive.

The humdrum of nine-to-five started to deliver grown-up stresses to our relationship, and the problems society predicted would follow began to fog my rose-tinted glasses. We started to bicker over even the smallest and most insignificant matters, and conflict hung heavy in the air.

One cold night in May, I was home alone when Max returned from a boozy night at the pub. My pregnancy was now nine months along and my due date had passed. I found no humour in his drunken state, and he clearly wasn't charmed by my interrogation tactics. As he zigzagged towards the bedroom, we exchanged words...

In a fit of hormonal rage, I stormed out of the house – barefoot and still in my Dumbo the Elephant nightie – slamming the door behind me.

'Fuck, fuck, fuck,' my teeth chattered as I tip-toed like Bambi in a Dumbo disguise through six inches of snow.

As the snow turned my feet blue, I concluded this was no place for a heavily pregnant and scantily clad woman. I turned to go back indoors before realising that, in my fit of anger, I had left the key inside, and the door would have automatically locked. I banged on its solid wooden panels to no avail. More banging and shouting proved futile as Max had clearly passed out.

I walked around considering my options and eventually spotted a ladder resting against a wall in a neighbouring property. My stairway to warmth was soon propped up against the wall below our second storey bedroom window. I climbed up barefoot to rattle the window and get Max's attention. Balancing precariously on an ice-covered top rung, I could see him sprawled out on the bed, dead to the world, as the hangover of tomorrow busily prepared itself in his body. I banged on the panes, I called his name, I cursed him, but mostly I cried, as he lay comatose.

Frozen to the bone I could think of just one solution. I walked to the nearest payphone, dialled the operator, and by reversing the charges, I was able to call my long-suffering mother. She didn't take too kindly to being woken at two o'clock in the morning, but the dutiful mother in her kicked in. Within half an hour, she had driven over with my spare key and let me in. Not a word was spoken – not a word needed to be spoken – her face told me I remained a 'silly, silly girl'.

Once inside, I shook Max awake and tried to start another argument. He slurred through a combination of drunkenness and drowsiness that it was my fault for going outside, and I yelled back that he was to blame for getting drunk and falling into such a deep sleep. My happy ever after was crumbling.

In May 1988, almost two weeks after the baby's due date, I casually strolled into my employer's office as the work week came to its end, to hand in my resignation. Without the marbles to know that I was eligible for maternity leave, I was tossing it all in.

I felt rather pleased with myself when the woman in HR who received my notice expressed surprise.

'You are doing such a good job and have a bright future in the payroll department,' she assured me.

My happiness levels shot up even further when I announced that I was about to have a baby, and she did a double take.

'Oh, my dear, I would never have known,' she said. 'You aren't showing at all.'

I suddenly felt this strange responsibility sweep over me. I would be a mum at any moment. I would have a dependant, and that meant I needed to get another job as soon as possible after the baby's birth. For some puzzling reason, asking the HR woman if I could return to work after the birth didn't enter my head.

However, I contemplated many other employment possibilities, even re-applying for the first-ever job I had at the tender age of fourteen. It would mean a return to arming myself with bulletproof yellow gloves and clinging to an industrial loo brush, as it entailed cleaning the men's room at a local factory for an hour each day. The activity invariably coincided with several workers needing to relieve themselves in one of the eighteen urinals that lined the walls. They hardly gave me a second glance while I was down on my knees, cleaning their mess as they hauled out their meat and invariably re-splashed my just-cleaned floor. I wasn't embarrassed – this was normal to me. And who was I to complain when they were creating my employment?

Luckily, I had a strong work ethic drilled into me from an early age. Work didn't scare me. My father had often said that it isn't luck that makes us succeed, but hard work. However, job thoughts were quickly set aside as my waters broke in the small hours of the day I left my job.

Max had a Yamaha 50cc motorbike – fondly known as Fizzy – as neither of us was old enough to drive a car. Despite the capability and reliability of Fizzy, we concluded that carrying a pregnant woman in labour the fourteen or so miles of country lanes to the nearest hospital in Newmarket was bordering on insanity. We didn't have a home phone, but my knight in shining lemon-yellow Kappa T-shirt armour dashed around to the nearest payphone to call my parents and tell them they had to take me to the hospital.

It had been months since I had any direct communication with Dad. We hadn't spoken, and neither of us had made an attempt to reconnect. We both seemed content with the decision, but now circumstances were forcing us together. He was coming to my rescue and taking me to hospital for the birth of his first grandchild. Dressed in the same Dumbo the Elephant nightie I had worn the evening of the lockout ladder incident, I slowly walked to Dad's car and opened the back door. He gruffly commanded, 'Make sure you sit on that old bath towel I've put on the seat.' What did he expect, Niagara Falls?

The journey to the hospital was undertaken in stony-faced silence. Mum occasionally turned around to check on me but said nothing. My only source of amusement was Max, trailing us and clowning around on Fizzy. I wished I was on Fizzy too, for even with its many shortcomings, it was a far preferable option to sitting on that towel in Dad's brooding company.

On arrival at the local hospital, the brewing verbal volley between father and heavily pregnant teenage daughter was placed on hold as I was promptly wheeled away to an awaiting medical team. I saw Dad as a monster, but he wasn't. He was just a pissed-off parent, rightfully exasperated with his certifiable nut-job child. I was the know-it-all epitome of every father's nightmare. Yet, in that moment, I felt incredibly alone and afraid, and I desperately wanted my mum and dad in the examination room with me.

The mint green walls of the room were so thin that I could see the outline of my parents in the adjacent waiting area. My fear was interrupted by the arrival of a rotund, old-school and no-nonsense midwife. She extended her right hand and introduced herself while looking me over with her judgy examination eyes. She asked me to lie down while simultaneously pulling on a pair of clear latex gloves and proceeded to direct me, 'Chop, chop, raise your knees, put your heels together and splay open your legs like a frog, please Mrs, or is it... Miss?'

I wasn't sure what splay meant but she firmly showed me by guiding my youthful pins into place. After a short internal examination, she pulled off her gloves in an officious manner and left the room. Being underage, any procedure required my parents' consent, so they had to receive a detailed debrief on my medical condition before we went any further. Max wasn't there, as he'd picked up a puncture while swerving to miss a rabbit and had gone off to get it repaired.

'Could you two please step in here for a moment,' the scary examination nurse said as she poked her head out of the room and around the corner so she could eyeball my seated parents.

My parents' faces were etched with pain as they looked up. The mortifying start to the day was about to be surpassed. The nurse took the half-in, half-out-of-room stance in front of the three of us, coolly and calmly saying, 'Yes, I think it's amniotic fluid, but it could be semen!'

There's a quiet resilience that emerges when life demanded more from me than I thought I could give. It was in these moments of struggle that I discovered how much I could endure. Above all, I learnt that we are never truly alone when we have strength growing inside us.

4

Class Act

What do you do when your father looks at you as if you've just unleashed a family secret in a public waiting room and proceeds to choke on fresh air?

Dad could not look me in the eye, let alone talk to me, and Mum just froze like she'd been turned to stone by the snake-haired Medusa midwife. It felt like I was in one of those weird movie moments, where everyone's drugged and in a room that is spinning out of control. Everything then abruptly stops, and someone's face magnifies, becoming the sole focus. In my case, it was Dad's.

In the nick of time, a saviour in the form of a trainee nurse arrived and whisked me away to the labour ward. I sat in my wheelchair, labour-pain free, and contemplated why everyone seemed to think the pain of childbirth was such a big deal. Then the first of the contractions hit me like a thump to the stomach with a sledgehammer. Many more followed in reliable succession and all with increasing ferocity.

My decision to forego ante-natal classes left me totally ill-prepared. I had not bothered to read up on what lay ahead, reassuring myself that this giving birth lark would be like taking the cork out of a bottle.

'Give me some fucking drugs,' I screamed as I was struck by another contraction.

Things weren't panning out the way I had expected, and I started to levitate from the bed like a scene from *The Evil Dead* and take on the voice of Lucifer himself.

I was mid-chant when Max returned. Through my red, bulging eyes, I spotted his orange puffer jacket, which had guided us into this mess in the first place. My knight in shining armour had taken the trouble to get kitted out and was wearing his most stylish gear to welcome the arrival of his first child. My adoration soon dissipated as my eyes fell on something brown in his hand. The knight in shining armour moment was replaced with me flying through the air at his throat, as closer inspection revealed him casually hanging on to a box of KFC.

There I was, screaming my head off, and about to pass the equivalent of a fucking watermelon, and there the tool was, casually munching on a chicken leg covered in the Colonel's secret herbs and spices. I do not recall what I said next, but my exorcist impression must have been powerful stuff, as the nurse told me to watch my language while simultaneously cooling my forehead with a flannel that, I suspect, she had soaked in holy water while holding a crucifix.

Not going to the ante-natal classes also meant it was a surprise to me that when you have a baby, you are likely to empty your bowels. Without any warning, I did just that, and poor Max was there to see every pebble. His facial expression contorted to the point where a sizeable piece of chicken dropped from his mouth in tandem with a turd that raced, neck and neck, to the floor. At least it stopped him eating his KFC.

The overhead lights and numerous sets of wide eyes beamed down on me as the medical team shared encouragement and instructions. A relentless series of world-ending contractions followed before the agony gave way to ecstasy brought on by a meek wailing.

The next chapter had officially begun. I was a mother, and a tearful Max was a father. Max kissed me on the forehead and whispered, 'We have a son, and he has your huge big toe.'

As I held James to my body, I could feel his little beating heart, and

I marvelled at the peach-like white fur that covered a head way too large for his little body – there was no doubting who his dad was...

Max and I both cried as we looked over this perfect creature – head size notwithstanding – and in that moment, for the first time in our lives, we realised someone was more important than us. For a split second, life was again perfect.

My parents dropped by a little later in the day to meet their first grandchild. Mum brought a lovely soft blue toy dog, and I watched intently as she bent down over the crib and placed a kiss on James' forehead. She went on to gently lay the gift beside him before telling me he was beautiful.

Dad looked on with a smile on his face. He was unable to mask his feelings when engaging with the newest edition to the family, but he still couldn't look me in the eye. It was clear both Mum and Dad were well aware that life had got a whole lot harder for their little girl – even though I was blissfully unaware.

Placed in an open hospital ward, my privacy was limited to a sage green curtain that divided the space either side of my bed. Magically, my body had sprung back into shape almost immediately, so I was back to being skinny – how cool, I thought.

I insisted on spending every waking hour in the nursery, looking at James amongst the mass of other not-as-cute babies. My constant fussing over him had the nursing staff nickname me 'Proud Mum'. 'Proud Mum' was also 'Grateful Mum' when I learnt that the woman alongside me, separated by only the sage curtain, had tragically lost her child at birth the day before. I felt guilty for asking her to stop her persistent wails the previous evening when I was trying to sleep.

The woman's tragedy had a profound impact on me. I felt sad for her and blessed at how fortunate I was. I could not imagine anything worse than something bad happening to my boy. I had instinctively moved into motherhood and being his protector.

The entire birth experience, while faint-worthy painful and somewhat inconvenient, was free from complications. Birth did leave my nether region looking like it had been put through a mincer though, not to mention leaving me singing like an opera singer whenever I took a piss.

Discharged within a matter of days, I stepped out into the harsh reality of teenage motherhood. Old friends had moved on during the pregnancy, and I did not fit in with the much older than me new-mum crowd pushing their strollers through the streets and engaging in endless baby talk.

However, even though we as a couple were probably not emotionally ready to raise a child as a couple, we somehow got by. James wasn't going to die through neglect or lack of love, and he was a well-cared for boy.

Caught up in the dream of a wonderful family life, Max and I contemplated the next logical step of marriage. It would complete the circle, even if our humble status meant the event would be a low-key affair at a registry office. Built on the rickety foundations of immaturity, our impending marriage had all the ingredients for failure. We still assigned enormous importance to Diamond Back BMX bikes and Kappa T-shirts, with our shallowness playing out in daily arguments, largely about things that hadn't happened yet.

'I think we should call off the wedding and end the relationship,' I flippantly ventured one evening as Max vacantly stared into the abyss of any object that wasn't me.

This was a threat I had thrown at him most weeks since we had moved in together, and his response was always to leave the room. I would invariably await his return, and resume arguing until he fell asleep. This time, although a flippant comment, I knew deep down that I meant it. There was no defining scenario that tipped me into the decision. I just instinctively knew that our nineteen-month-old happy angel deserved better. James needed to be free from incompatible parents who would be happier apart.

The first call I made the next morning was to my parents, asking if they would meet me at my favourite place for a walk – Wandlebury. The day was one of mixed emotions. I was filled with joy to see James running ahead with his blond locks bouncing up and down, almost disappearing in the long grass. Thoughts of what might lie ahead as a single mother, still in her teens, left me sad and frightened. As I walked alongside Dad, I serendipitously shared three life-changing words with him. 'I'm leaving Max,' I said.

Dad reached out, and with a soft touch of his working-man hands, he took my arm and swung me round to face him. He looked me straight in the eye and asked, 'Do you want to come home?'

Dad looking me in the eye was something he hadn't done since before the evening I had left my parents' home for what we all thought was the last time. Despite all the issues of the past, the perceptions of who was right or wrong, and debates over who had screwed up whose life, I didn't hesitate to say a heartfelt, 'Yes!'

It was a huge sense of relief as I pondered this being the start of the rest of my life. I felt sixteen again, ready to erase the turmoil of the previous couple of years and gain control of my future. Dad knew my existence would be a train wreck if I remained in an unhappy relationship, and he was quick to tell me he would be around to collect me and my worldly possessions – a son, a cot, and a front-loading washing machine – the very next day.

Back at my parents' home again, I knew it would be a short stay, the exact length determined neither by me nor my parents, but by the availability of a council house. That was my goal from the moment I proudly wheeled my front loader into my parents' garage. I felt this Carlton washing machine signalled my rise from the 'social-handout class' of twin-tub owners to the far loftier status of 'working class'.

I knew it was my parents' wish that my stay was short too – who could blame them. And I wanted my own place with James, away from what I saw as disapproving parents who were quick to remind me that I remained a 'silly, silly girl'. In their eyes, I was a lodger who didn't give emotionally to them. I paid rent of thirty pounds per week in return for a bedroom for me, one for James, food for both of us, and a roof over our heads – the arrangement was purely functional. Never once did we sit down and chat about my time with Max, how we had gone about raising James, how we felt about each other, and what led to the souring of the relationship. Nor how I, or they, felt about the Friday night two years earlier when I had sprinted from their lives.

We did not indulge ourselves with prodigal daughter stuff. In our household, the golden rule was that you never raked over old coals. There was nothing to be said. I was there simply because it was better than hanging out in the increasingly toxic relationship Max and I had cultivated.

I must confess, my new living arrangements were a good deal. The state gave me sixty pounds a week as a single mum, and I had my parents to baby-sit James, which freed me up to take a string of part-time jobs to supplement my government allowance.

Employment came in many forms as income was always my priority, and I never refused any job offer, including a stint as a cashier at a service station and the occasional house-cleaning job. This helped to cover the rent, as well as the copiously consumed alcohol that was becoming a big part of my self-absorbed social life. To further augment my income, I delivered Yellow Pages at ten pence a pop. I transported the books in my first car – a hand painted blue Opel Kadett Dad had bought for my eighteenth birthday for a princely price of sixty pounds. Loaded to the roof with heavy yellow phone books, I often did the rounds of Haverhill with the Opel almost on its two back wheels with the windscreen facing skywards.

Dad and I got along famously as he was away all week, and I made myself scarce on weekends. It was housebound Mum who bore the brunt of having a teenage daughter and a young child around the house. I drove her insane with outrageous babysitting demands that would allow me to work some days, go clubbing most nights, and spend a lot of time sleeping.

Once a week, I would join the zombie-like benefits queue at the local post office, where I stood shamelessly for hours while rocking James' pram and proudly displaying him kitted out in Nike, which in my world was designer clothing.

Of little or no help around the house, I saw it as my parents' responsibility to provide for me and babysit James. I gave little thought to their lives or how I might be an imposition. There was no internal struggle as my life was unequivocally all about me. All I wanted was fun, money and a man. And, while I pursued my mid-life crisis at the tender age of nineteen, Mum and Dad took care of the rest, including James.

On one of the infrequent occasions that I did try to thank them, I monumentally stuffed it up. When Mum and Dad treated themselves to a rare long weekend break, I decided to show my appreciation for everything by repainting the magnolia walls in their home. I could picture the result and see the joyful surprise on their faces as they returned. I could hear them thanking me for my kindness and praising my painting skills that rivalled those of Michelangelo. I would make the ceiling of the Sistine Chapel look bog average. This brilliant idea had come to me after a chance meeting with two guys in a nightclub while we were all under the influence of speed, at least I think that was what it was. I invited them back to my parentless family home for a drink or two. As we chatted through the night, the conversation veered towards what we all did for a living. Luckily, they went first as I would have had to fib about my not-so-stellar professional credentials. They indicated that they were painters and decorators. Handy, I thought as I looked at the tired walls through my massive drug-infused pupils that magnified every flaw.

'Would you guys be up to helping me repaint my parents' house?' I ventured, and in their altered consciousness, they gave me a convincing thumbs-up.

With brushes and paint purchased from the local hardware store the following day, the boys and I set about the job knowing that we were up against the clock with the weekend ending and my parents about to return. Way out of our depth and drowning in a sea of paint, we rushed around to produce a patchy and botched job that was destined never to reach acceptability.

Dad was the first through the door that Sunday evening and immediately his jaw dropped along with his suitcase. Rooted to the spot and rendered speechless, he scanned the walls. I saw the blood rush to his face in a re-enactment of the night he returned from the doctor with the news that I was pregnant. But he said nothing – he just stared at the walls with the expression of a stunned mullet. Then my mother came through the door.

'Who the hell do you think you are? Whatever possessed you?' she screamed.

The two clowns I had befriended at the nightclub had long disappeared. They turned out to be rookie apprentices who clearly should have considered other careers. Within days of completing the paint project, I heard on the grapevine that they had been supplementing their legal income and had been picked up carrying a sizeable stash of drugs. They went on to serve time at Her Majesty's pleasure and thankfully, I never heard from them again.

Shortly after the paint episode, I was taught another harsh lesson – Horticulture 101, *Don't mess with anyone's pride and joy without their permission.* Dad's garden was his oasis where he would spend many hours in solitude and be at one with nature. He had a knack for creating something special in the garden, and top of the list was a lovingly cultivated grassy knoll. The knoll rose from the lower level of the garden to deliver a fine-manicured look to the upper level. Even though this *pièce de résistance* was already resplendent with a verdant covering of lawn, I thought a little trim would add to its appeal. While he was away on one of his weekly lorry-driving trips, I dragged out the lawnmower, only to find my mowing skills matched those of my painting. I hadn't grasped how tricky it was to manoeuvre a lawnmower with its various blade heights over hilly terrain. I could feel the glide wasn't silky smooth but continued to walk the full length of the garden before turning to find a scalped brown fifteen-inch strip all the way down the middle of the lawn. I had beheaded the full length of Middle Earth, leaving its top savaged, arid, and broken.

'Oh shit,' I said, while gormlessly transfixed on the vision in front of me.

Dad's homecoming after a hard week at work elicited a similar response to the one following their long weekend away, only this time the meltdown was in the garden. His high-pitched screams must have caused all the windows in the neighbouring properties to rattle, and they were masterfully accompanied by what looked like breakdancing across Middle Earth. While impressive to observe, it was clear to me that I had messed up again. I was clearly still a fucking idiot.

It was fascinating to me that I had spent so much time trying to protect myself from the world, only to realise that it was in those moments of shared fragility that I felt more connected, more human – even when all I wanted was to hide and hope it would all go away.

5

Siam... Please

It's not every day you find yourself tangled in a web of celebrity hookups, a yellow sticky house, and pupils so large you can see through your eyelids. But then again, my life was never what you'd call ordinary. By now, you'd understand why celebrity hookups were high on my list of goals, but let's just say coming face-to-face with violent gerbils? Not so much.

With so much self-inflicted anarchy around, I increasingly found refuge in men. And as the song goes, it was raining them. Ravers at nightclubs, itinerants passing through, any nice-looking one would do. They came and they went in quick succession – and I unashamedly had no desire to settle down. I had got that T-shirt a few years earlier and I was now determined to do what I should have done at sixteen, and it wasn't going to stop anytime soon. All relationships were of the here for a good time, not a long-time variety. I was living my youth without a care in the world.

Independence was still a top priority, which meant finding a house for me and James where I could get on with my self-absorbed life without the disapproving glare of my mum and dad. I walked the housing estates on most days to check out the vacant council houses. I would jot down their addresses and take my list to the deadpan you-ain't-getting-a-house-on-my-watch ladies at the local council office. I assumed they had nothing better to do than listen to me and heed my every request. I suggested they give me this house... or maybe that one... or perhaps even that one.

Embarrassingly, one of these ladies was Timmy's Mum, who gave me a look that suggested she shouldn't have bothered to chastise him for standing me up on that disco night. She probably thanked her lucky stars that her only son had the wisdom to escape the clutches of this benefits beauty as opposed to a beauty with benefits.

After six months of badgering, I called into the council offices and was told a house on my vacant list would soon be allocated to me. Yippee! I would be on the move again – this time leaving my parents' home in a sedate and orderly fashion.

My hand-painted Opel Kadett spluttered into life, with James snugly in his car seat in the back. His second-hand two-foot six-inch single bed and my treasured front-loading washing machine would follow in a kindly neighbour's trailer. I waved a mutual thank-fuck-for-that farewell to my parents and headed the mile across town to my new Chalkstone estate home.

'Oh God, what a shitpit,' I said as I pushed the front door open and looked in on an old and distinctly orange dwelling.

Almost knocked backwards by the pungent mix of stale tobacco smoke and nicotine, I had a new appreciation for why so many had re-christened my hometown with the unflattering moniker of Haver-hole. I concluded there was no way any place could smell like this unless the previous occupants smoked continuously from every orifice.

Standard council house eight-inch square matt black and mostly broken floor tiles covered the floors. Lines of nicotine stains snaked down the walls, windows, and doors. The white wood that once framed each window was now blackened and crumbling with mould. It was the stuff of nightmares. Disgusting but aptly my shitpit in Haver-hole.

I set about turning the shitpit into a palace – my palace – and called in favours from the men in my life, including Dad and Max. In a scene reminiscent of the Industrial Revolution, an army of men laboured in horrid conditions. Some were down on their knees replacing floor coverings with the carpet sample squares I had bought for ten pence each from a local carpet shop. Others scrubbed every nook and cranny of the house with the huge scrubbing brushes Dad had kindly donated to the project. Still others set to work repainting the walls with an assortment of leftover paints generously provided by my parents' neighbour. A new cooker was purchased, along with a small second-hand fridge/freezer and a dream sofa from the local department store. Its hire purchase bounty of twenty-six pounds sixteen pence per month for four years made it my single biggest ticket item. With no income worthy of note, Dad stepped in to guarantee the loan. I measured up the windows and made my own curtains from bargain offcuts. They looked fantastic as surprisingly I had paid attention during needlework classes at school. A dining room table was deemed an extravagance – James and I would manage on our laps. Gardening equipment, cutlery, crockery, pots, pans and linen were all supplied by an army of well-wishers.

Now transformed into my home, I loved it. It was spacious, with three bedrooms, a bathroom, two toilets, a lounge, a kitchen and a dining room. Downstairs was an inviting, warm cocoon I could share with James.

Of course, like all council homes of the decade, there was no upstairs heating. Each step to the upper level took the visitor into the mythical world of *The Lion, the Witch and the Wardrobe* and the arctic wastes of Narnia. This was a world where your breath would fog as you exhaled. The silver lining was that we didn't need to buy pens and Post-it notes. We wrote notes for ourselves on the condensation on the windows each night, comfortable in the knowledge that they would be there in the morning as frozen reminders.

My conflicted world was neatly compartmentalised. Behind the front door I was a single mum with a modicum of respectability and responsibility. But when I was roaming on the outside, I was a reckless, free-as-a-bird good-time girl. The challenge was how best to deal with my two existences and ensure they never collided.

I lived like the husband with two wives, where the double life is led so well that the only person aware of the duplicity is the one in the starring role. They do it well for years with the truth finally emerging at their funeral...

Just like the two-timing husband, there was a clear line between the two versions of me and never the twain would meet. While I didn't give James a model upbringing, he was always clean and well-presented, with a tummy full of food.

What happened on tour stayed on tour – and there was plenty of touring, as good fortune delivered me a great next-door neighbour.

Julie was the epitome of the 2.4 children family. She was a warm and house-proud mother and wife; her hardworking husband was the breadwinner and they both doted on their two beautiful daughters. Her maternal traits meant she was only too happy to add James to her brood whenever my clubbing addiction took hold. She was a model mum and selfishly, she became my liberator.

My double life enjoyed a distinctly double week, with the responsible period stretching from Monday to Thursday. I would take James to school each morning and collect him again at about three o'clock. In between, I was mum and housekeeper, taking an interest in his schoolwork. During school hours, I would bolster the meagre social handouts by tackling any number of menial ad-hoc part-time jobs.

The setting of the sun on a Thursday evening rapidly transformed me into a party animal and held me voluntarily hostage until Monday's recuperative session. London was my preferred destination, heading there with any girlfriend keen to party – and there was no shortage of those in my phone book. On the rare occasions when I had no takers, I would happily go out alone and head straight for a favourite location in London's West End with the intention of bagging a rich male celebrity. I *may* have signed a Non-Disclosure Agreement or two while hanging out at the most 'in' place of the day, a club named The Emporium. Suddenly, I was rubbing shoulders with George Michael and Naomi Campbell and convincing myself that I was on the cusp of a life I thought was long overdue.

Monday was designated recovery day, with me lying on the sofa, slipping in and out of consciousness and feeling decidedly rotten. My head throbbed, my parched mouth was unquenchable, and my ability to care for James limited to basics only. It was at those moments the good mother James didn't have and absolutely deserved was exposed.

How was James to understand that Mummy had just spent the best part of the last seventy-two hours in the gluttonous rave and recreational drug scene? I didn't want him to know about this dark and sweaty world where people off their faces and dressed in dungarees and silly hats would blow whistles while bouncing around the dance floor for hours on end. And always, there were the strangers who would slip and slide their way through the throng of young revellers.

'E's, E's,' they whispered.

They would rack up ecstasy sales that turned their consumers into apparitions of the cartoon dog, Muttley. Ecstatically happy and aroused, with oversized pupils dripping intoxicated tears onto their clenched jaws. The grinding teeth of revellers sometimes drove them to chew on black rubber bathroom plugs they had pinched from the toilets.

I, James' mummy, was part of this lost bunch of sub-humans in search of ecstasy, speed, and whatever else was on offer, and it was as far removed as humanly possible from what I hoped my son would be doing in *his* twenties.

There was one occasion when acid became the drug of choice following a week of being particularly skint. A visit to a nearby nightclub provided the perfect platform for its test flight. New to the drug, I was given a quarter-centimetre square tab, which would have a street value at the time of around three pounds. I recall thinking that this little piece of paper couldn't give me a buzz. A friend more seasoned in these matters assured me I had plenty and suggested I break it in half. As you'd expect, I ignored the well-meaning advice and placed the entire tab on the back of my tongue, where it dissolved.

The gerbils arrived en masse. They were everywhere, the rascal rodents running amok, and some of them even travelling in spaceships. The wind picked up and blew my flowing locks while the greedy gerbils tried to shoot me with Tommy guns. Amid the chaos, a friend who didn't yet have her driver's licence decided it would be safer for her to drive my car home for me. I curled up into a ball in the footwell behind the driver's seat, trying to shield myself from another volley of gerbil gunfire. The gusts of wind were now of gale-force proportions and blasting through my little Opel Kadett, which was quite remarkable as all the windows were wound up.

The next morning the nightmare continued, my eyes were firmly closed, but my pupils were able to see through my eyelids. Worse still, I could see gerbils in my bedroom. Increasing their arsenal to weapons of mass destruction, they had colonised every inch of my room. I was terrified and swore then and there to never touch acid again.

I would have stayed hiding under the covers all day but for a pre-arranged medical appointment with the same young doctor who had confirmed my pregnancy.

A cold and wet mid-winter day, I arrived at the surgery wearing an Andre Agassi fluorescent orange headband, a flimsy T-shirt, a pair of shorts, bare feet and pupils the size of saucers. When I stepped through the door, the doctor said nothing, but I sensed he knew precisely what he was looking at and what I had been up to. He was clearly disappointed that his predictions for me had come to pass. When the gerbils stepped aside to give me a clear line of sight, the sadness in his eyes was unmistakeable.

My weekend nocturnal habits also led to the same disapproving look from one of my elderly neighbours. He thought I was a lady of the night who supplemented her income by selling her body. Whenever I ventured out of my home, his curtains would twitch to catch a glimpse of my nefarious lifestyle. He had lost his wife a short while after I moved into my home and, although a rather opinionated fellow in his late seventies, he seemed lost without his life partner. Always smartly dressed in a sharply ironed cotton shirt, a pair of beige stay-pressed trousers and braces, his slight covering of silver hair added to a debonair look. I could hardly blame him for his presumed opinion of me, as I was undoubtedly a selfish fuckwit.

In a strangely ironic way, I was first on the scene some years later when he suffered a heart attack. I had been hanging up the washing when a loud and purposeful knock on my front door told me something was amiss outside. I opened the door to find a middle-aged man and his Labrador dog. The man didn't say hello or offer any other niceties, instead frantically yelled at me to call an ambulance.

'I have just seen an elderly gentleman collapse in a heap right outside your house, and he doesn't look too well,' he added.

I knew instinctively that the unwell man was my elderly neighbour. I called an ambulance, grabbed the nearest available warm covering – James' Thomas the Tank Engine quilt – and rushed out to wrap him up in the warm bedspread. It was a bitterly cold winter's day, the frost lying thick on the ground around him. As his skin had already turned grey, I knew his chances of survival were slipping away. A wave of sadness rushed over me as I commenced CPR on him. While we were not friends, he had been a familiar face in my life and had been interested enough to have an opinion of me. I also felt conflicted about how disappointed he would be if he knew that the last lips he ever locked onto were mine.

Poor fellow, I thought while looking down at his lifeless body. He must have already left planet Earth when I lowered myself onto him to try to save his life, as you can be sure if there had been even a hint of a pulse, he would have jumped to his feet and slapped the local lady of the night for trying to seduce him.

I quickly rummaged through his pockets in search of his house keys as the ambulance arrived to take his body away. Jumping to my feet, I ran to his house to find a picture of his beloved late wife. There was a beautiful one on the entrance hall table of them both smiling on a park bench. I placed the picture, still in its frame, under his shirt. He was now with her, in heaven, at peace, and there was nothing more for me to do other than wave the ambulance staff farewell as they drove away.

The Thomas the Tank Engine quilt was now soiled and deposited in the nearest dustbin. I stood in silence as I reflected on the sadness associated with the end of a human life and then the difficulty of hatching a credible story to explain to my son how his beloved quilt and the elderly next-door neighbour were now inextricably linked in the afterlife.

Back on earth, my chameleon skills, which had the first part of the week being seriously at odds with the last, extended to another area of my life – how to better my financial situation with the minimum of effort. Money was tight, even though my welfare now provided me with sixty-three pounds each week. My occasional part-time positions supplemented the balance with an additional fifteen pounds and allowed me to stay afloat without accruing debt.

Clubbing was largely free. I would drive friends to the various raves, and they would reciprocate by paying for the car fuel. Sidling up to and engaging in some small talk with anyone from the opposite sex invariably led to the charging of my chemical fuel. I had no problem with my approach because as I saw it, I had two choices: I could use the only leverage I had – my looks – or I could go without.

I went on a date with some poor sod solely because he was able to connect my cooker for free. Another useful association fixed my gas boiler gratis too. A plasterer chipped in and a plumber too, while another unsuspecting chap serviced my car.

I morphed straight into damsel-in-distress mode when in need of a favour. My long curly hair would be worn down and softly draped over my right shoulder, with my slightly tilted head adding the finishing touches to my pretence.

One day, I decided my love for cats needed to progress from the stream of moggies that had snuck into my life in recent years to a posh pedigree.

'Hmmm, I do like the look of Siamese cats,' I said to James, while lazily paging through a cat book one evening.

Strategic dating kicked in again as I sought out and found a nondescript boy whose mother just happened to breed Siamese cats. The poor unsuspecting fellow looked every bit like the cats his mother bred. He was very skinny, with a face that looked like it had been sucked out of a passenger plane at thirty-three thousand feet. But I got my cat.

It seemed like nothing was beyond my single-minded determination to get what I needed, regardless of how selfish it was. My way of trying to fill gaps I didn't fully understand kept me from seeing the bigger picture. I was fighting a battle with myself, even though it was hidden behind a smile and lots of partying. In the end, it wasn't the things I collected or the shortcuts I took that mattered – it was the relationships I missed while I was too busy building walls instead of bridges.

6

Shit Parcel

Why is it, the more I tried, the more my world sucked? Are we sometimes so blinded by what we want to believe that we fail to see what's actually there? What does it take to wake up from the illusion? Or, in my case, get rid of the shit, before it's too late.

While on a two-week holiday in Greece, accompanied by a friend and with James in tow, I discovered that nothing could rein me in, not even geographical boundaries. Still a rash and reckless holidaying single mum, my sole objective remained to meet a gorgeous rich man and live happily ever after.

As I lay on a glorious beach and watched the sunlight dance off the shimmering water, there he was, emerging from the surf less than one hundred yards away. My Greek God – blond, tanned, toned... and heading my way. He approached me and smiled as he plonked himself down on the vacant real estate left on my beach towel. He was beautiful, Adonis-like, and I was instantly madly in love. Two blissful weeks with Georgios, known as George, followed before I returned to the UK with a heavy heart. I had just said goodbye to a magical fortnight where I was the centre of a man's world – not just any man, but a dreamy Adonis who was falling in love with me. He was great to look at, and he showered me with compliments and adoration for everything I did.

After my holiday romance in Greece, my mind raced with thoughts of George as I struggled to return to the normality of life in Haverhill. I even started to think about how I could get him a visa – our love would be enough to bring him to the UK and we'd hold each other close forever. George assured me his feelings matched mine and was quick to back this up with daily phone calls, each one brimming with his undying devotion.

With each call, my spirits lifted, as did my belief that this was it. This was for real. The emotions we shared surpassed anything I had ever felt before, and I was certain I had finally found 'the one'.

One evening, during one of our calls, George suggested that I should pop over to Greece for another visit. I didn't hesitate. I rushed to the nearest travel agency and within a week, I was stepping through customs at Athens Airport, straight into his waiting arms. 'How fucking brilliant is this?' I shouted, before his lips silenced me with a long, passionate kiss.

Even the long train journey to Thessaloniki, where we picked up our transport for the week – a Robin Reliant three-wheeled car belonging to George's father – couldn't douse the flames of excitement. Neither did George's erratic driving, as he careened into the city's peak hour traffic, darting across lanes and swerving into the nearest petrol station. He turned off the ignition and the little engine spluttered, shaking the car as it died. As the silence settled, he broke it with a cryptic announcement that he had a secret to share. Maybe he was actually going to ask me to...

'I'm engaged to be married,' he blurted.

I think he went on to say that he had real feelings for me and while he would be tied up with his fiancée during the day, he would very much like to see me during the evenings. I heard little more than a drone as his opening volley had left me momentarily in a parallel universe and unable to communicate with the real world.

'You are what?' I eventually responded in a pitch so high it was likely only animals of the canine variety could hear me.

George got out and filled the tank from the bowser before extending his hand and gesturing at me to provide the money. Stunned and bewildered, I offered a fistful of cash, while wondering how I could still be in this game. My ego told me I could share him for the time being, slowly wow him, and eventually win him back.

While George pranced around during the day as the supposed faithful fiancé, I consoled myself lying on the beach like a stray puppy. My forlornness didn't go unnoticed as a young Greek family introduced themselves during one of their late afternoon strolls. Even with the language barrier, a friendship of sorts blossomed. A few days later, in a gesture of kindness, the wife approached me holding a large white envelope, which she gently placed at my feet. 'A gift from Greece to you,' the woman murmured shyly.

I slowly and purposefully opened the envelope to find a large red ticket with Greek writing on it. I studied it closely but was none the wiser.

'Notis?' I asked, being careful not to sound ungrateful.

In her mostly broken English, the woman informed me that this chap Panagiotis 'Notis' Sfakianakis was Greece's answer to George Michael – his concerts were sell-outs, and his voice like no other.

With nothing else to do, I made my way to the concert that evening. It was in a cavernous Colosseum-like outdoor theatre, heaving with music lovers waving still-to-be-lit complimentary sparklers, which no doubt would add a dash of visual brilliance to the show.

My attempt to endear myself to my newfound Notis friends plummeted when the host stepped onto the stage. He trotted out with Greek greetings and announced that the support act was *Fairground Attraction*. Just as Notis meant nothing to me, this good old British outfit did not register with the locals, so their appearance received only a polite hand clap. Not even the belting out of their signature hit, *Perfect,* roused the mostly moribund audience. In stark contrast, I jumped up onto my seat, lit sparkler in my hand, and sang along in what I thought was close unison. Woe-is-me tears rolled down my baby-oil-instead-of-sun-cream fried cheeks. Alone and a touch sad, I was nonetheless very proudly British!

By the time Notis finally stepped onto the stage, my sparkler had well and truly fizzled out. My enthusiasm for the rest of the night was just as limp. I could only sit there, tears streaming down my face, as thousands of excited Greeks climbed onto their chairs, holding their sparklers aloft. The dark sky lit up as the audience sang and swayed, lost in the magic of the night.

George visited me at my hotel each evening as promised, eager to be of service... One night, he went even further, inviting me to join him at the nightclub where he worked behind the bar.

'I'm on duty so won't be able to hang out with you,' he announced in a matter-of-fact tone before adding that I could sit on the corner stool at the bar and feast my eyes on him and his bartending performance.

'George, you're such a twat,' I shot back. My eyes did a quick scan of my barely-there hot pants and ample braless breasts behind a flimsy top. 'You see me as nothing more than a blonde Brit night-time trophy you can show off in front of your barmen colleagues – don't you?'

George didn't reply as I continued to watch him, resplendent in his black trousers, starched white collared shirt, and natty Aladdin waistcoat. Lust told me to stick around and see what might transpire, but my pride eventually kicked in.

'Fuck this for a date,' I muttered to myself as I gulped down the last of a nasty cocktail, then slid the empty glass across the polished wood counter. With a swift spin on my heels, I marched towards the nearest exit.

George was engrossed in raucous conversation with a few of his colleagues, oblivious to my departure. I stepped silently into the dark night, took a guess at the direction, turned left and began wobbling down a deserted, winding rural road in my four-inch stilettos. The path, more goat track than road, stretched on for what felt like miles, and I hoped it would eventually lead me to my dingy hotel.

'I hate you, George,' I mumbled unconvincingly, as I stumbled homeward, my feet protesting every step.

A little way into the journey and snivelling loudly at my misfortune,

I heard a rustle behind me and turned sharply to see a stray dog emerge from the bushes. Had my orchestra of melancholy moans attracted a new mate? Maybe he had heard me a few days earlier when I had learnt of my Greek God's two-timing?

Seconds later, the sole canine was joined by a pack of his mates.

'Fucking outstanding, my life just gets better,' I cursed, a sudden shiver of fear creeping over me. A primal sense of being hunted surged through me, re-igniting my will to survive. Without looking back, I quickened my pace, my stilettos threatening a blowout if I went any faster.

The stray dogs responded by striding ever closer until they were alongside me. I could feel the warmth of their panting on my bare legs as fear overtook me, and tears began to fall. The thick, damp air from a recent rain heightened my anxiety, and then, through the fog, I saw the outline of a man approaching, a black garbage bag in hand. Gripped with fear and filled with thoughts that my life would end on some deserted Greek road; my mind ran into dark places while imagining my final moments. The garbage bag was the dead giveaway. His outline suggested he had a large physique, someone who would hardly raise a sweat overpowering me and placing the bag over my head. Not satisfied with suffocating me, I would be raped while I took my last breath. The ravenous wild dogs would revel in eating my corpse. I would simply disappear, only to return as high carb dog shit. No one would ever know what became of me, the happy-go-lucky young woman who had jetted off to Halkidiki for a lovers' reunion...

I cranked down my wailing, putting on my best I-have-grown-testicles-and-an-Adams-apple voice, in the hope that the psychopath passing by would mistake me for a cross-dresser and think twice about messing with me.

The man's shuffling footsteps grew louder, getting closer until I could make out his features through the fog. I wasn't wrong. He was big, rugged and definitely on the seedy side, looking like the kind of guy who shows up on a *Crime Stoppers* e-fit.

Instinctively, I clenched my fists, ready for the life-or-death struggle that was surely coming. But before I could land one of my legendary blows, the pack of dogs changed formation. Half a dozen veered left, the rest right, encircling me in a protective formation that felt impenetrable. Step by step, they marched in sync. Mr. Seedy passed by without incident, and the dogs fell back into line behind me, escorting me like a security detail.

When I reached my dimly lit hotel, the lead dog stopped and watched me as I pushed open the door and stepped into safety. By now stone-cold sober, I turned back in disbelief. The dogs turned back and disappeared into the hot Greek night. I was struck by the feeling that they had cared more about my well-being than I had.

'Perhaps I have a greater purpose in life that I am yet to discover?' I stammered as I shook my head in doubt and shuffled off to bed.

The one-week holiday from hell dragged on according to George's script. His days were spent with his fiancée, his evenings consumed by work, but his bewitching-hour charm always found him in my bed – if only until his needs had been satisfied.

Everything changed on my last night in Greece. George suggested we spend it in his parents' apartment, as a regular train service ran from their neighbourhood to the airport and his parents were away. I considered turning him down. I knew I should have. But in my confused, love-struck state, incapable of distinguishing between reality and fantasy, I foolishly agreed.

'Yes, that sounds perfect,' I said, clinging to thoughts that there might still be life in this relationship.

The apartment was located on the top floor of a seventeen-storey building, immediately opposite the lift lobby. Compact, clean and modest, it featured two bedrooms, a lounge, a kitchen/dining area and a bathroom. The décor was a vibrant reflection of Greek culture, history and tradition. Cream-tiled floors were adorned with a scattering of brightly coloured handmade flokati rugs, while minimalistic dark wood furniture, carved with geometric patterns, was carefully arranged throughout. Classical motifs and intricate tapestries adorned the walls, adding to the cultural charm.

Directly opposite the entrance hallway was the small kitchen, where a window offered a birds-eye view of the neighbouring high-rise buildings. To the left, the hallway opened to a modest lounge bordering George's parents' bedroom. A large display cabinet filled with glass and brass ornaments dominated one wall, with a collection of ornate candlestick holders taking pride of place. Across from the lounge was a small bathroom, equipped with a shower, basin and toilet. At the end of the corridor was a cramped box room with a single bed wedged into the corner – clearly, this was George's bedroom.

Dusk was falling as we settled down to an early dinner in the form of a bean casserole his mother had lovingly prepared for him. I had not had the satisfaction of a decent shit since leaving the UK and nervously eyed the meal. But I was starving so I cautiously consumed every morsel on my plate.

The meal instantly began fermenting in my stomach, no doubt stirred by a vigorous session of post-dinner hanky-panky. Afterwards, George announced without fanfare that he was off to bed in his room and that I should make myself comfortable in his parents' room.

It was around three o'clock in the morning when I awoke in a panic, jumped up and ran to the bathroom. My stomach was churning, and a volcanic eruption was on the rise. While I thanked God George had made the fortunate decision to sleep in another bedroom, I knew I needed to act quickly.

My rudimentary knowledge of Greek society and customs told me that toilet paper wasn't thrown down the loo but rather placed in the somewhat undersized – well, for what I was about to deliver – bin provided. There was also a complicated manual flushing system that

I knew wasn't going to be man enough to handle what I was about to serve up.

My dwindling options caused me to reflect. Here's this guy I love that I'm trying to wrench from his fiancée's arms. I haven't had a shit for a week and the gravity-fed loo requires me to fill up a bucket of water and wash it all down. I can't put the toilet paper in the bin, and I don't have a front door key that will allow me to escape and drop this impending mother lode elsewhere. If I go about this in the intended fashion, I will surely awaken my one true love. He will, on seeing the forest of toilet paper in the bin, know I have dumped a massive British turd in his parents' home. Not romantic!

With my insides now rumbling uncontrollably, I clicked into survival mode. Muddied by love and its uncanny ability to remove logic from the equation, my addled brain concluded the solution lay, quite literally, in my hands.

If I gather a load of loo paper, place it in my cupped hands and position them strategically just below my bum, I can shit freely, confident that the flow of excrement will land safely where I want it to. I ripped yards of toilet paper from the roll and positioned myself expectantly.

The initial fart was immediately followed by a massive booming volley of weighty brown faeces and, while the manoeuvre had been perfectly executed, I was now confronted by an even larger challenge. How the fuck do I effectively dispose of this mammoth mound of steaming turds?

It was enormous, weighty and wet too. In fact, it was rapidly turning the toilet paper into a sloppy mess that could no longer contain its load. Fluids were now cupped in hands carefully positioned, palms up, still under my backside. I considered myself pretty good at yoga, especially as I took in the sight of all fingers pointing, with purpose, towards my butthole.

Unable to change the angle of my hands for fear of spilling the unstable mass, I somehow managed to shuffle crab-like through the house with my knickers around my ankles, my destination being the kitchen window.

Determined not to wake Prince Charming, I carefully manipulated most of the slop momentarily into one hand and wrestled with the for-fuck's-sake-open-from-the-top-and-pull-inwards window, which was clearly designed to stop kids from falling out, and presumably, fuckwits from flinging out shit.

The window creaked open, releasing a waft of warm air. Triumph was just a flick of the wrist away. Consumed by immense relief, I juggled the load back into two hands, stood on my tip toes and flung the whole catastrophe out the window. I crept back to bed feeling much lighter on my feet and filled with a huge sense of achievement for my first-rate crisis management skills.

When I walked into the kitchen the next morning, my eyes were instinctively drawn to the window. A wave of fuucckk washed over me. My paper and turd pie had nested snugly on the outer window ledge. And, worse still, it had splashed the unthinkable all over the windowpane as it came in to land.

'What the fuck,' I mouthed. Panic returned as I realised George must have seen it and known that it could only have come from me, as there were no apartments above his parents' home to blame it on.

I trawled my brain for plausible explanations to offer George when the inevitable question was asked. Perhaps it could have been an aeroplane emptying its toilets on the flight path towards Athens? Then again, there must be a reasonable, if only slight chance, that an albatross, having just consumed a large bowl of beany dog food, had crapped itself empty on the windowsill.

Surely, my Greek God would choose to believe one of these scenarios before thinking that this beautiful English Rose was responsible. However, neither explanation accounted for the trail of shit drips that led from the bathroom to the kitchen – much like the breadcrumbs to a gingerbread house. Surprisingly though, he said nothing and didn't point the pooey finger at me. Maybe he somehow hadn't noticed it after all?

I was certainly not about to draw his attention to it. Instead, I retreated to my room to prepare for the journey home, emerging half an hour later dressed in my trendy white linen outfit, reminiscent of something you would find in the wardrobe of Sonny Crockett of *Miami Vice* fame. George dutifully drove me to the train station in readiness for the last leg of what had been a disastrous trip.

To my surprise, George decided to accompany me on the train. As with most public transport in Greece, the train was hot and crammed with passengers, almost all of whom were locals in their customary black attire. The crush of bodies only heightened my discomfort, and in my crisp all-white ensemble, I stood out like a sore thumb. I reached over to slide open the window, hoping for a bit of fresh air, when an elderly Greek gentleman suddenly grabbed my arm.

'No... no... noooo,' he advised me in broken English, shaking his head and sharing his concern with fellow passengers.

I ignored the overwhelming show of support he had from the other passengers and just offered up an I've-got-this-covered smirk while giving the window a solid tug. The next thing I remembered was waking up on the floor of the train with a sharp pain accompanied by a large gash to the top of my head. My once-pristine white linen outfit was now stained with a mix of blood and dust. George, along with half a dozen locals, stood over me, staring.

'That guy was only trying to help you,' George ranted. 'He told you not to open the window because kids are known to throw rocks at passing trains, but you always know better, don't you?'

I opened my mouth to argue, but then I saw George's serves-you-right-for-shitting-on-my-window-ledge look, so I wisely decided to keep my mouth shut. To add to the unfolding scene, the blow to my head had somehow loosened the remaining semi-digested bean casserole from my lower digestive tract, and it had ejected into my trendy white linen pants. I somehow managed to smile, and allowed my thoughts to roam towards getting to the airport, dumping my shit-filled knickers, boarding the plane, and leaving this literal shitstorm behind.

At the airport, I finally reached the security area with George walking behind me. As he stepped through the metal detectors, a penknife in his pocket set off the alarms, triggering an almighty commotion. I stopped dead in my tracks and swivelled around to see a posse of menacing-looking security officers swarming over George while he struggled to wave goodbye and plead his innocence at the same time.

My last image of George was him being frog-marched away by two enormous security guards, headed who knows where for who knows what. Maybe he was destined for a Greek version of *Midnight Express*? Maybe a cavity search? I smiled at the thought. A cavity search seemed like the perfect retribution for his treacherous betrayal.

Maybe ridding the world of a total twat was my greater purpose in life? Perhaps that was why the wild dogs had kept me safe?

With a sense of finality, I strode towards the departure gate, hoping to leave behind a memory that had been nothing short of shitful.

I didn't need to have it all figured out to find my way. The mess, the mistakes, the challenges – they were all part of the journey. With every fall and every failure, I had to remind myself – this isn't the end, it's just the beginning of the next chapter.

7

Gobble, Gobble, Gobble

How can a ridiculous bet in Magaluf become a defining chapter in one's life? It's where the lines between pleasure and purpose blur, and where the pursuit of fleeting gratification reveals unexpected ambition and valuable life lessons. Amidst this, a complex dance between self-interest and connection starts a journey of transformation.

Having left school at sixteen and determined to fulfil the promise I made to myself that the first book I ever read would be the one I wrote, I found myself with no qualifications to offer employers. Consequently, my job prospects were bleak and limited to menial work. I didn't need a fancy diploma to apply for house cleaning jobs, as I was already skilled in the craft, so I channelled my efforts in that direction.

It wasn't long before I was offered a position as housekeeper for a successful civil engineer. Recently widowed, he needed help with nearly everything, including caring for his two daughters and son while he was at work. Though he was busy, he was considerate, and his children were old enough to be well-behaved, which made the job easier.

The steady work environment allowed James to accompany me during the school holidays, giving us more time together and saving on the cost of childcare.

Between my housekeeping duties, I was able to take on other roles. I worked as an assistant florist, crafting an array of bouquets for all occasions, from births to funerals. I also had the occasional waiting shift at a local café and worked as an administrative assistant, where the mind-numbing tasks included listing the adhesive properties of sticky labels – semi-permanent for this batch, permanent for that. None of it required much skill.

As Christmas approached, I took a temporary position as a sausage packer on a production line at the local meat factory. Standing at my post, I watched the sausages come down the belt, ready to be caught. In a single movement, I lifted the sausages from the belt and with a samurai move, flicked them into a bundle of eight. I then placed them on a little bracket on a fast-moving conveyer belt, ready for packaging by someone down the line. To break up the monotony, I engaged in playful banter with my co-workers and even had fun flicking a sausage or two around in light-hearted moments.

I was surprised to learn that when the six-week contract was up, I was deemed unfit for re-hire. The supervisor explained that my cheerful demeanour was considered a distraction and negatively affected productivity.

'You are too jovial for a work environment that requires focus,' the supervisor told me during my exit interview.

One of my other roles was to sell Avon cosmetics via mail order. Being an Avon Lady was simple – I bought my catalogues from Avon, packed them in little plastic bags and walked the length and breadth of the housing estate, dropping them into letterboxes. A week later, I'd return to collect the orders or if someone wasn't interested, hopefully get my catalogue back. With my sales skills being rudimentary at best, the orders dribbled in. Since it was commission only work, I earned a grand total of eight pounds a month, which went straight into my money pot that was strictly reserved for buying birthday and Christmas presents for James.

Canvassing strangers gave me new insight into human behaviour and how to deal with its many foibles. Some people were lovely – others not. Some would quite literally tell me to fuck off. I could take the unpleasant behaviour, but I struggled with not getting my catalogues back as each represented money, which was in short supply. One occupant of the not-so-nice variety returned the catalogue with hand-drawn knobs on every page. I guess that meant they thought either I, or Avon, were dicks – meh, who cares? I wasn't about to clarify it with them either way. Despite the paltry earnings, Avon ultimately served as a springboard to the next chapter in my life – learning how to connect with strangers.

The many jobs I had enabled me to save enough money for a much-needed holiday with a girlfriend called Tina. I trusted Max to take care of James for the week at his home while I indulged in the attractions – human and otherwise – of Magaluf in Majorca, also known as 'Shagaluf'. It was there I met Mike, a Club 18-30 representative.

For those unfamiliar with Club 18-30, it was a holiday company catering to the eighteen-to-thirty age group, offering packaged excursions focused on wild parties at some of the Mediterranean's biggest party hotspots. In the 1990s, it proudly embraced a promiscuous image in its advertising, gaining notoriety for cheeky slogans like, *'Get up the crack of Dawn... or was it Julie... or...'*, the racy *'It's not all sex, sex, sex... there's a bit of sun and sea as well'*, and the truly inspirational *'Gobble, Gobble, Gobble...'*, for those lucky enough to visit a resort in Turkey.

I loved what Club 18-30 offered – its unapologetic hedonism and bold focus on pleasure. Mike, with his short red hair, blue eyes, chiselled face, and athletic build, was a prize catch. But it was his husky voice that ultimately bowled me over. Our relationship lasted all of one night – or more accurately, twenty minutes, which included a catnap.

In that fleeting moment with Mike, I was exposed to a world of totally uncommitted sex for the first time. Just sex. Sex for fun. Not sex with a side order of 'let's see where this goes'. It was liberating and carefree – very 'hippy' – and I felt good about it. I revelled in the celebration of the body, the rejection of traditional gender roles, and the freedom that came from the idea of an open relationship – what Gen Z now call a 'situationship'.

Moral considerations aside, the days were filled with flirty energy and willing Club 18-30 suitors were everywhere. One day by the pool, Tina glanced over the top of her sunglasses at me and threw out a challenge. 'I bet you'd make a great Club 18-30 Rep!'

That was all the encouragement I needed. It was clear to me that joining Club 18-30 offered a rare chance to have fun and make some money. I figured that if I worked for them, it would be limited to a summer season, during James' school holidays. He could easily stay with Max, and I'd be back before the new school year started in September. The depth of my decision-making process lasted all of one evening. I was going to become a Club 18-30 holiday representative, and nothing was going to stop me.

I returned home and applied for a position with the organisation for its upcoming summer season. My application was enough to get me onto a shortlist of candidates who were invited to an interview weekend in Manchester.

Seasoned managers from the various resorts sat in the audience of a large auditorium while we hopefuls walked onto the stage to be judged much like at a Crufts Dog Show. The managers would glance up from their notebooks, assessing each candidate's stage presence, talent, charisma and, I imagine, our looks. Competition was fierce as I went head-to-head with hundreds of likeminded, egocentric candidates all striving to secure a spot on the path to paradise.

The managers made their selections and the chosen few were now bound for exotic destinations while the hordes of less fortunate folk were politely told to seek excellence elsewhere. Translation: Fuck off.

I have no fucking clue how I made the cut, especially since I ended up performing a karaoke rendition of *Mustang Sally*... a song I had never even thought about before the interview. As the microphone was handed to me for my two-minutes of fame, I knew I had to go all out.

Mustang City, when you gonna slow that Mustang down? Mustang City now baby, when you gonna slow that Mustang down?

I figured I was doing alright, as the audience shouted what I assumed were words of encouragement.

I'll never forget the surge of joy I felt when a guy named Joe called out my name. It turned out that Joe thought my version of Mustang Sally 'City' was hilarious and a great approach to get the audience revved up. I never did let on that I didn't know the words.

I was happy with the pairing, particularly since Joe managed a stunning seaside resort in Turkey, which would be my 'gobble, gobble, gobble' themed home for the summer of 1996.

Arriving in May, I adapted quickly to the unfamiliar environment and new role. The warm, sunny days of early May were the perfect prelude to the chaos of mid-summer, when tourists flooded into the resort. Within just a few days, my new colleagues had already nicknamed me 'Barbie'. I chose to take it as a compliment – after all, she was hot, slim and blonde. In truth though, I was basically just a ditzy blonde. Still, for the first time in my life, I felt a sense of professional accomplishment, as though I could be good at something beyond house cleaning.

While most of my new colleagues were younger than me and there for a carefree, wild summer, I was a little different. My single mother status fuelled me with an unrivalled motivation to make money. With one eye on the fun side of things, the other was firmly focused on saving every penny I could.

The salary package was largely commission only. It meant I might earn diddly squat, but the perks were solid – free hotel accommodation, meals and unlimited alcohol. I wasn't going to starve, and the more tours and merchandise I sold, the higher my earnings would be.

I quickly became super competitive, highly motivated and perhaps even ruthless at times. I was comfortable talking to complete strangers and I mastered the art of negotiation – willing to do almost anything to gain a sale. I also became well-equipped to handle the variety of issues that arose during people's holidays, even the occasional tragedy. Through it all, I built trust with the guests, who were more than willing to part with their hard-earned cash in exchange for the excursions on offer.

The twice-weekly airport runs were where it all began for the newly arrived holidaymakers. I would meet my fifty or so guests at the airport and load them onto the bus for the four-hour drive to the resort. With their undivided attention, I would cruise up and down the aisle introducing myself and making small talk. I went out of my way to answer any questions they had, ensuring they felt valued and getting them excited about the fantastic days and nights we had planned for them.

Salivating at the prospect, I delivered my *magnum opus*. 'All you need to do to live the dream is purchase our tours...'

It never failed. My old credit card machine – the franking version – whizzed back and forth for much of the journey and the sales commission kept climbing.

I always adhered to the golden rule that holiday Reps must respect the 48-hour exclusivity embargo on each other's hotel grounds. During this time, we weren't supposed to encroach on our colleagues' turf. After that, it was a free-for-all with anyone selling to everyone. Some Reps frowned on the practice, deeming it unfair, while others weren't bothered. The girl from Haverhill wasn't bothered – I wanted every possible sale and was prepared to enter anyone's territory to sniff out more business.

My competitive streak was matched only by a hotelier who had decided to invest in 100 desktop fans for the hotel rooms, as they lacked air conditioning. I supported his initiative, thinking it was nice of him to make the lives of the tourists more comfortable as they battled the stifling Turkish heat. However, my gratitude was short-lived. Two weeks later, when the first batch of revellers were due to leave, the hotelier posted hefty hire fee invoices under their doors. The uproar was immediate, with the indignation deep enough to have the Club 18-30 guests refusing to pay. But the hotelier stood firm, insisting it was a legitimate fee and that it would be a criminal offence to leave without settling the bill. A standoff loomed, tempers flared and despite my best efforts, my negotiation skills came up short.

The hotelier was resolute, barking his final word on the subject. 'If you don't pay, you don't leave Turkey!'

So, my holidaying British guests were forced to pay. It was sad that their final memory of an otherwise great holiday was of draining the last of their bank balances. With slumped shoulders, I ambled slowly and miserably to the local strip of bars to drown my sorrows.

'Why the long face?' one of the bar owners asked as I rested my face on the counter. I shared my shitty day story, along with the deep disappointment I felt towards the hotelier whose behaviour had forever tarnished the reputation of Turkey's tourist resorts.

Upon return to the hotel later that night, I walked past the swimming pool and noticed a rather unusual scene of the hotelier and about ten shady-looking men sitting around a long table deep in discussion. In the gloomy light, it bore all the characteristics of a mafia gathering. A chill ran down my spine when one of the men caught my eye, winked, and flashed a toothy grin that reminded me of Al 'Scarface' Capone.

Up early the next morning to start work, I was surprised when leaving the hotel, as parked out front was a shiny new moped, wrapped in a big bow. It had a card dangling from the handlebars carrying my name. The untidy inscription told me it was the hotelier's gift for me and his peace offering.

It wasn't until a week later that I learnt that the gathering around the pool *was* of the don't mess with us sort. My bar rant had clearly spread through the local grapevine and reached the ears of the town's wheelers and dealers. They had frowned upon the hotelier's greed, and appreciated how negative the impact could be on the resorts. The local mobsters demanded that he make good by treating me like a princess. After all, I was the darling Brit who was bringing lots of tourists to the bars along the harbour front and generating a large amount of revenue.

Now having a moped meant my treks to the not-so-near hotels to capture any missed sales were easier. More importantly, the moped meant I could increase the frequency of visits to the phone box three miles away to call James.

Amid the random chaos of resort life, I found myself in the arms of a colleague, Samuel. We had fun together. He helped fill the void of loneliness, offering companionship without commitment, yet somehow, it felt oddly committed. It was a connection based on the moment – a brief escape from the emptiness that lingered when the lights went out at the end of each day. We were all young, all far from home, all missing our families.

My fellow Club 18-30 Reps became like family. We shared a bond forged in the unique craziness of our roles, and that connection felt as though it would last a lifetime. But beneath the glittering surface of my carefree life, there was a loneliness I couldn't shake without James at my side. People would come, people would go, and in the blur of fleeting faces, we used each other for the promise of two weeks of gratification, knowing it would all end just as quickly as it had begun.

It was a world built on temporary highs, and I was caught somewhere between the euphoria and emptiness, constantly seeking something to fill the space inside me that no amount of partying could satisfy.

I came to realise that temporary escapes are not distractions, but lessons in self-discovery. More importantly, I discovered a fulfilment that didn't depend on external validation, but instead, gave me a quiet strength to stand alone.

8

Golden Showers

Have you ever locked eyes with a stranger who you have an overwhelming pull towards and found yourself at odds with what you thought your future would look like?

Within weeks of my return from Turkey, I reunited with my colleagues at Club 18-30's annual reunion at a hotel in Blackpool. The venue was packed with excitable young Club Reps from across Europe, all brimming with energy, mischief, and of course a hippy-characterised approach to sex.

As the event was winding down, I entered the lift and made eye contact with a guy who flashed an intriguing smile. We exchanged a few pleasantries as he introduced himself as Jeff. Before I had a chance to respond, the lift doors opened, and I was again alone.

To my delight, Jeff shared my bus back to London the next day. We exchanged numbers and I knew I would see him again. Though he was not my usual type, there was something about him – his sense of humour was infectious, and I found myself getting butterflies whenever I thought of him. What followed was a high-octane, intense seven-week romance akin to something from the screens of *Married at First Sight*. We even travelled abroad for an intimate weekend in Istanbul, where much of the time was spent playing a wild game of 'Never-have-I-ever'.

Straight in for the kill, Jeff grinned mischievously and said, 'I dare you to give me a golden shower.'

I paused for a moment, then responded in my usual never-back-down-from-a-dare tone, 'Okay, but I don't know if I can wee with you watching me...'

'Start filling up on the fluids and when your bladder is at bursting point, bingo,' he suggested, his grin widening. 'You then get on top and piss all over me – simple!'

I'm not sure I ever understood the sexual appeal of being pissed on. It is very hard to pee on someone when your every move is being watched. It is doubly hard to have sex with a person you have just pissed all over too. But I won the dare...

Forty-eight days after our chance meeting and no longer able to suppress my happily-ever-after thoughts, I boldly invited Jeff to move in with me. To my delight he said yes. It was a significant moment as no one apart from James and me had ever lived at our home. I had been ultra careful that whoever came into our home lives would be there for the long haul. I didn't want to introduce a man into James' life only for him to walk away. James wasn't going to be a boy of many 'uncles' and grow up thinking it was normal to bail when the going got tough.

Jeff arrived the next day with a suitcase bursting at the seams. We passionately embraced and immediately shared thoughts of a future together. Lying on my lounge floor, we gazed into each other's eyes and pledged our undying love. Marriage seemed inevitable, with a tribe of little ones running around the house. We even found a scrap of paper and a pencil, and together we designed my engagement ring.

We spoke of creating a loving home and finding responsible and 'proper' jobs. Uncannily, in tandem with our conversation, the letterbox rattled suggesting someone had posted something through it. It was a weird twist of fate as I'd never had a newspaper posted through my door before and never did again. It must have been delivered to my house in error, but I grabbed it and we both lay on the floor giggling like lovestruck teenagers to browse the job section.

My eyes zoomed in on two jobs I felt confident we could do. One was for a prison officer and the other for a flight attendant with Virgin.

'I can already see you strutting down the aisles of an aircraft serving coffees,' I giggled at Jeff.

He grinned and said, 'I dare you to apply for the prison officer job.' He playfully poked me in the ribs, with a glint in his eyes.

The challenge had been set, and I hedged my bets by applying for both roles. Jeff agreed to apply too, but only for the prison officer job, and we mused about how we would be real adults, with proper nine-to-five jobs. We went to bed in each other's arms, dreaming of settling down to domestic bliss.

'Jeff,' I called as I awoke seven hours later and stretched out a loving arm only to find his side of the bed cold and empty. The silence was broken by the *Power Rangers* movie playing from James' bedroom. 'Jeff, mine is two sugars, please,' I shouted, expecting him to pop in with a smile.

I thought nothing of it at first. Jeff was a prankster, and this was just another of his shenanigans. I headed downstairs expecting him to jump out and surprise me. But a full search of the house failed to find him or his suitcase. I felt sick in the pit of my stomach – Jeff had done a runner. He was a free spirit and deep down, I knew the look in his eyes the night before was one of doubt. Club 18-30 was in his DNA, and he was not ready to face the enormity of growing up. Right then the phone rang. I picked up the receiver and heard his unmistakable voice. He was calling from a public pay phone at Gatwick Airport. 'I'm sorry,' he slurred through his intoxication, 'I love you, but I need to get back to Majorca. I'm only young once, and I need to have fun. I will love you forever.'

And with that, he was gone.

I collapsed to the floor in melodramatic self-pity, my head swarming with questions of what I'd done wrong. Heartbroken that my husband-to-be had vanished, I immediately went into 'I must make this work' mode, even though that had spectacularly failed me years before with the

Greek God. I should have known to leave it there, but my ego wouldn't allow that.

Six weeks later, still desperate for Jeff, I arranged a short visit to Majorca. I knew it would be a disaster – I had been a Club Rep, so I was well-versed in its key performance indicators. He wasn't in a monastery pondering his recently taken vow of celibacy. No, he was a slick operator, partying hard and no doubt tangled in a web of one-night stands. Yet, despite my first-hand knowledge, the voice inside me kept insisting this was a special relationship worth fighting for.

I flew out to an inevitable distant reception at Palma de Mallorca airport, which only confirmed my gut feeling. It also gave me a steely resolve to get through the holiday and make sure I partied hard. Defying good judgement, I latched onto the first good-looking guy I came across – a bloke from the west of the UK. I never got to ask him his name as he was in my life at that precise moment to serve two purposes only – provide me with some distractive fun and cause pain for Jeff.

The next evening, with all the Club Reps, including Jeff, up on stage performing as only Club Reps can, my drunken west country loudmouth acquaintance stood up and pointed to my ex on stage and yelled out, 'I shagged your missus last night!'

The audience of intoxicated youth laughed before starting an *I shagged your missus last night* chant that went on to become a holiday mantra for the men, a bit like a football song.

I shagged your missus last night, I did, I did, I shagged her proper, I did, I did. Followed by the chorus, *You're not singing, you're not singing, you're not singing anymore!*

With bridges well and truly burnt, I fully embraced my role as the party girl of the precinct. I was the good-time girl who had casually shrugged off the broken relationship and was lapping up every moment of her newfound freedom. Jeff was not impressed, especially when one night in a bar I hooked up with a celebrity of the day who had recently split from another celebrity of the day. Our titillating playfulness ended with someone taking a compromising photograph of the two of us.

By that point, any hope of reconciling with Jeff was dashed for good. The Majorca interlude ended, and I feigned a dispassionate farewell to the man who had once been the love of my life.

My bravado was all fake. I was devastated and it took months for me to get over it, largely because my ego had taken a thrashing. Here I was, an attractive young woman who liked to be in control, yet I had been dumped – not just dumped, but dumped by someone who, in my mind, should have considered himself lucky to punch so high above his weight. Or so I thought.

My woe-is-me thoughts eventually turned to life beyond Jeff, prompted by a letter from the Prison Service advising that I was required to attend a shortlist interview in London. The next day, another letter appeared in the mail, this time from Virgin Holidays – and again the news was positive. While the flight attendant position was far more glamorous, I had already lost interest in it as it paid a thousand pounds a year less than the prison job. It was a no brainer. I told Richard Branson he would have to keep his planes in the sky without me! As a single parent with a sporadic and low income, money talked and the more I earned the more I could borrow to buy a house of my own.

I approached my prison interview in a similar fashion to my pregnancy. I knew bugger all about the Prison Service, I knew no one who worked in prisons, and I had not been in one myself. My comprehension of prison was based solely on the *Prisoner Cell Block H* series. I didn't really have any desire to tread that path, so I didn't bother to research the role or prepare myself for the looming interview – after all, it was just pure chance that *The Daily Telegraph* had landed in my hands.

On the day of the interview, I boarded the train to London wondering why I didn't feel nervous. Everyone had warned me of the angst I would face with my first-ever 'proper job' interview. But anxiety and apprehension were completely absent as I cheerfully bounced in to confront an austere three-person assessment panel. A rotund, considerably older male governor sat in the middle, flanked by a stern, scary-looking woman and a softer, more welcoming female governor. The room matched the sombre atmosphere – sparse and devoid of warmth, save for a few pieces of outdated furniture. The long bank of tables behind which the panel sat, only added to the coldness.

I immediately identified my chair – the lone, unoccupied piece of furniture slap-bang in front of the panel – a little like the electric chair on death row I thought.

The male governor, Hank, had a look of bemusement. Upon seeing me bounce into the room, he suppressed a little chuckle, or at least I think he did. The other two remained stone-faced, maybe stunned into silence by a candidate who was a little different from those who had presented to them that day. They detected an individual who had never been serious about anything, and who was distinctly unsuited to a career that demanded the utmost discipline. Even when the questions were fired at me, I took them in my stride and treated them like I would a bit of old banter in the pub. I didn't think about another 'too-happy-to-employ' note being dropped into my job application file. Hank was mostly silent for the first part of the interview, while his two colleagues bombarded me with questions about my attraction to the job and my knowledge of prisons. Hank eventually joined the interrogation after staring at me for a few moments.

'So, tell me,' Hank said, his voice steady. 'You walk down a residential landing of fifty cells and there before you are two of the toughest criminals you have ever set eyes on. They are beating the life out of each other. What do you do?'

I had no frigging idea. I couldn't call the police now, could I? I thought for a second and delved into my small reservoir of wisdom while simultaneously blurting out, 'Okay, what I would do is this... I would turn around and run in the opposite direction to make sure I don't get injured. I am physically smaller and weaker than these brutes and I don't fancy being stabbed to death on my first day of the job.'

With a nonchalant shrug I fixed my gaze on Hank and wondered how my answer was being received.

Hank leaned back in his chair, threw his head back and laughed – loudly. It was a deep laughter that started in the pit of his stomach and rose to a booming crescendo. His colleagues found nothing amusing about my answer, and once the laughter subsided, I casually asked, 'So that's not the right answer, I take it?'

He chuckled again, this time holding his bountiful tummy. 'It's an answer.'

I left the interview without a firm decision, which I took as a positive and an indication that my response to Hank's question had not been completely shite. The panel had not said yes – nor had they said no. They told me they just needed time to consider the other applicants, their strengths and weaknesses, what they would bring to the service and various other points I don't recall as apathy had by now well and truly set in. Hank did, however, drop a cheeky wink my way that I thought may have suggested I could expect a letter conveying good news.

I wanted a job, any job, and just like buses, if I missed out on this one, there would be another one before too long. With time on my hands and Jeff still on my mind, I hit upon the perfect solution that would kill two birds with one stone. I would give Jeff the middle finger by returning for a second season of Club 18-30 partying.

True to my word, in early summer I arrived on a beautiful Greek island to start my second season. One afternoon, a new colleague and I managed to get hold of a cassette tape of Paul McKenna, the world-renowned hypnotherapist. Lying on her bed, we hit the play button, stared at the ceiling and prepared for some serious chillaxing. McKenna's soothing words drifted into our heads and soon rendered us completely and utterly out of it. As luck would have it, the boss decided to drop by our hotel that day. Noticing we weren't at our designated work area – the swimming pool – he came looking for us. He eventually found us in a deep mid-afternoon hypnotic sleep and promptly woke us to the news that we would be docked a week's commission for taking a few hours off duty. He was a bit of an arsehole, but we devised a cunning plan to shorten our punishment. Brilliant in its simplicity, my colleague would pretend she was attracted to him to see if she could get our fines reduced.

I didn't dare ask exactly what she had to do for the penalty reduction, suffice to say, our fines were reduced to just one day's commission.

Despite the allure of a gorgeous Greek island and its constant partying, I could not shake the melancholy that had descended upon me since Jeff's cruel departure. Feeling lonely and sorry for myself, I called home to talk to my mum about the weather, and she mentioned there was a letter waiting for me, sealed with a Government crest.

'Open it, open it,' I screeched down the line.

Mum played along for what seemed like ages, telling me to relax as she slowly and purposefully opened the letter. I held my breath as I heard the envelope rip apart before Mum announced that it was from the Prison Service. I had been offered a position as a prison officer. As the reality sunk in, I was overcome with emotion. I was delighted that I had landed a proper job. Conflicted, I turned around in the payphone booth to the familiar sight of bare-chested and hot young Greeks, with a picturesque and sunny Mediterranean island as their backdrop. In a panicked attempt to refocus, I dialled Jeff's number to share the news and asked if he had received any mail.

'I don't know why I applied for the job,' he said. I could practically hear him rolling his eyes while chewing gum. 'I have no desire to work in a prison but if that's what *you* want, go for it,' Jeff concluded before abruptly hanging up the phone.

I was to report for duty on November 3rd, 1997. The timing couldn't have been more perfect. I had always made sure I could take James to school for his first day of the new academic year. Simply walking him to school on that opening day in early September surely made me a good mother?

I had learnt that love isn't always about staying – sometimes it's about knowing when to let go. I wasn't very good at letting go. I hadn't yet figured out that love is about two people being on the same page at the same time.

9

Stomach Pumping

I was on the cusp of a real job, buying my first house and adulthood – a logical, responsible path. So, naturally being the fuckwit I am, I decided to squeeze in one last night of partying before buckling down. Instead of planning my 'in', I found myself kicked out – again...

The six weeks between James' return to school and the start of my new career as a prison officer gave me the opportunity to get my life into a semblance of order. With a full-time job, I could achieve my goal of buying a house. I spent most days speaking to the local council to get permission to purchase the council-owned house I was renting. I also visited several banks to enquire about a home loan.

Arranging childcare for James was next on my to-do list, as I would be based at Prison College in Wakefield, a town in Yorkshire, for the first three months of my service – several hundred miles from home. Thankfully, my parents said they would step in to help with James, along with my wonderful neighbour Julie.

That left me with the last entry on my list – to celebrate. This was to be my very last hoorah before real-life got in the way. I reminded myself that I was not going to have any regrets when I went to bed on the night of November 2nd, 1997.

Much like the condemned prisoner gets to choose their last meal, I had the chance to choose where I would party on my last night before full-time employment kicked in. London's West End was calling, and it was there that I reconnected with a female guest from my Club 18-30 stint in Turkey. She was about six-feet tall, stunning and by definition, a complete and utter bitchface. She shared my taste in men and during her two-week holiday, had managed to bag a very hot barman. He clearly had eyes for this Elle McPherson lookalike rather than me, leaving me to bide my time and await her departure before I could pounce on him.

I arranged to meet a guy I had a one-, or two-, or maybe three-night stand with some months prior and we hit a nightclub called Caesars. The fifteen-pound entry fee included unlimited alcohol, which I thought was very civil of them. I wasted no time throwing back the first of many vodkas laced with Malibu and lime. The rest of the night rapidly became a blur.

The nightclub chapter ended with me having my face peeled off the toilet wall and being forced into the back of a cab by a very angry looking bitchface frenemy. I vaguely recall seeing my one-nighter – or was it two or three, in the cab, although I think he had his tongue in bitchface's mouth. I can't vouch for that as my vision was somewhat impaired, made all the worse by regular volleys of flying carrot chunks.

I woke up in a hospital bed with a very handsome young doctor disapprovingly injecting anti-emetic drugs into my bum cheek. My boob tube was covered in a mixture of black charcoal stomach pump stuff and carrots – very alluring... not. There was no way I was going to successfully hit on this rather fine-looking intellectual, so I just had to put it down as a missed opportunity. My nightclub friends were nowhere to be seen and through an intoxicated haze, I was somehow able to call my then London-based brother for help.

Saying little in response and sharing the odd disapproving laugh at his witless muppet of a sister, he performed his sibling duty and collected me. He brought several blankets and a pillow and gently placed me in the back seat of his car. Once at his apartment, he made sure I had a shower, plied me with water and headache tablets to fight the inevitable aftereffects, put me to bed and promised to never say a word about it to our parents.

The bedside alarm clock broke the sound barrier at half past five in the morning, just a couple of hours later. 'For fuck's sake,' I moaned as I rubbed my eyes, sat up in bed and took a where-the-heck stock of the surroundings. My mouth tasted like a cat's litter tray, my hands tremored and my stomach was concave, rather odd considering the liquid I had consumed the night before. As memory blearily returned, reality sunk in and I realised it was time to get up. How on earth was I going to get to work for the first day of my new grown-up job?

That was the first time I noticed the dutiful gene of my mother emerging in my older brother. I had left my car at bitchface's house as I had planned to drive to the training facility in Suffolk. My brother however, had no intention of letting me drive in my still hazy state. He insisted we take the train from his place to hers, and then he drove me all the way from London back to Haverhill. Once we arrived at my home, he waited patiently for me to change before dropping me off at the training facility in Suffolk. Then, without a second thought, he took my car back to my house, went for a leisurely jog the seventeen miles to Cambridge, and caught the train back to his home in London. His quiet, steadfast support in that moment made me appreciate, perhaps for the first time, how grateful I was to have him as my brother.

'What, no men?' I groaned as I arrived at the Prison Training Centre to find that the other forty new recruits were also women. Detecting my dismay and perhaps even overhearing my comment, a new colleague informed me that it all had to do with addressing the Prison Service's gender imbalance.

'Where the hell did it say that in the terms and conditions?' I asked rhetorically.

Our first meeting of the day was an orientation session with Hank. I recalled my interview and thought it appropriate to wink at him as I entered the hall – after all, we were besties. He raised his eyebrows in an unimpressed and disapproving fashion, and I was confused. What had happened to our friendship? Was I now little more than a female statistic?

It wasn't long before the old Hank emerged, and he told me that he would never forget my interview. He said it made him laugh, and that I was the only person on that tedious day of interviews who had brought a smile to his face. He went on to give me some advice: 'You have to promise me that you will never change, because it's important that you laugh every day at work.'

Hank's words meant a lot to me, as did his punt on someone who was most probably certifiable. So much for that 'too happy at work' comment at the sausage factory!

Hank was my first professional guardian angel. A strong, confident man of legendary standing at the prison, he owed his status as much to his professional prowess as to his liking of pranks. Rumour had it that during a football match, he had pissed in the winner's trophy instead of filling it with the traditional optics line-up from the bar. The poor bastard who took the first victorious sip immediately realised what he had consumed, and all hell broke loose. I chose to believe the story as it made Hank sound a lot like me. It probably accounted for him having faith in an upstart junior screw, thereby changing the course of my life.

After an uneventful week at the Prison Training Centre, where we were taken through numerous housekeeping matters and given a potted history of the Suffolk prison, we headed north to begin our formal training.

The Prison College in Wakefield was a nondescript building resembling an old and somewhat neglected school. I approached the large glass front doors with a mixture of fear and exhilaration.

Returning to a learning environment sparked a wave of panic in me. I had long assumed my brush with academia had ended the day I discovered I was pregnant and left school. Now, here I was again, riddled with doubt about how I would fare after so many years in the non-educated wilderness. But those doubts were tempered by bursts of adrenaline as I thought about what the future held.

I entered the foyer of the prefabricated 1970s building, my eyes falling on the old carpet on the floor and its mosaic of liquid stains. In the distance, a bored-looking security guard sat at the reception desk. He oversaw my arrival via an automated, emotionless sign-in process. I waved him a cheerful goodbye and trundled up the stairwell to the first floor, selecting the third room on the right in the dormitory area.

I swung the door open to be slapped in the face by a stale, fusty surge of teenage boy's bedroom smells – damp, musty and distinctly uninviting. The single bed presented another challenge. I wasn't used to its narrow two-foot six-inch dimensions and the plastic waterproof mattress cover that not only makes you sweat through the night but rustles with every movement.

However, my spirits lifted significantly when I met my forty or so fellow students. I knew instantly that this would be a chapter rich with laughter, adventure and of course, men. I eyeballed a few kindred spirits who, just like me, were mostly on the lookout for fun.

The playground on our doorstep was the town of Wakefield, with its notoriety as one of the country's top party towns and awash with cheap alcohol. I struggled to contain my excitement as this was just the destination for someone who had supposedly bid farewell to endless partying when hanging up their Club 18-30 clipboard for the last time.

Between me and the graduation that would launch me into a full-time job – complete with the promise of independence and a home of my own – lay two four-week blocks of college, with a two-week practical training stint in a prison in between. But before I could reach that coveted finish line, I had some serious hurdles to clear. The most pressing was posed by a super critical and jaded teacher who was the undisputed world champion of the 'bellend' medal. He epitomised the old school prison guard and showed little liking for any of his students. Surprise, surprise – he seemed to reserve his deepest loathing for me. I was the antithesis of his universe

– a person too jovial for a world where discipline, order and obedience were paramount. His dislike for me reached a new high two-weeks into our training. With a sneer, he surveyed the class of fresh, eager students, then, his tone dripping with disdain he asked, 'So, which one of you rookies thinks you will be a governor one day?'

No one dared to speak. The room fell into an uncomfortable silence, as everyone stared down at the floor or out at some non-existent object in the distance. Then, unexpectedly, my right hand shot up – betraying me, driven by a mixture of rising frustration and a touch of defiance. His condescending, dismissive attitude towards all of us demanded a response, and this girl was going to let him have it. His eyes locked onto mine, and with the contempt that only he could muster, he spat out, 'Oh my poor deluded child, if there is one person in this room who I can say with absolute certainty has not the faintest chance of progressing to governor, it's definitely you.'

I didn't flinch. 'Thank you very much, sir,' I replied with a sarcastic politeness.

I dug deep, calling on every ounce of self-control to not say anymore. I reminded myself that a foul-mouthed retort would plunge me to his level and that even with my 'star-studded' life thus far, I had standards below which I would not descend.

His awfulness was thankfully diluted by the presence of another student who shared my warped DNA – a woman named Sally who occupied the bedroom next to mine. We became partners in crime, finding small but meaningful ways to navigate the absurdities of the training facility. One of our most ridiculous performances was provoked by the shared communal toilets at the end of the hall. It was far too inconvenient to make the trek in the middle of the night, so we decided to use the wash basins in our rooms. Juvenile? Definitely. Disgusting? Probably. But for us, it was a clever way to manage our time and, in its own way, a team-building exercise. A bang on the wall signalled our intention of turning frustration into fun. We'd gleefully announce our regular ablutions with the now-infamous cry, 'About to piss!'

The inevitable response would come: 'Wait for me, I'll be up on mine in a tick...' Tandem pissing, we called it – a testament to the undeniable truth that girls aways go to the toilet in pairs.

This worked well until one day while perched on the basin, it gave way and before I could stem the flow, the basin came off the wall. I crashed to the floor while showering the room in piss. It was awkward enough having to call the maintenance team out-of-hours – totally mortifying when the maintenance man gave me that don't-bullshit-me look when I said I didn't know how it happened, with the added giveaway of a distinct smell of urine in the air and Sally's laughter bellowing through the flimsy wall that divided our rooms.

One day, during a Powers of Arrest tutorial, I managed to smuggle out a set of handcuffs and hid them under my bed. Let's just say, they were put there for a rainy day...

What a coincidence, the very next day it rained... The classroom was alive with gossip about a hot male specimen at the college. Everyone who had seen him had a crush on him. Obviously, my crush was unrivalled, sparked at first sighting and set ablaze during a period when we recruits were required to do a few laps of the oval. He was at the start/finish line having sped ahead. I imagined him having a wonderful day out, scouring the talent encircling him lap after lap. I imagined he was allocating scores out of ten to all the females. I was not in the least offended, in fact, I was hoping he was thinking about me and all the sordid things we were going to get up to in the very near future. As I ran past, purposefully wiggling my bum and sticking out my boobs like Barbara Windsor in a *Carry-On* film, I detected a glimmer in my man's eye.

'I have cuffs,' I involuntarily blurted out into his ear as I panted past him.

With no action over the next week, I began to doubt my skills at getting what I wanted but reminded myself that such failure was not part of my reality. A few short days later, while my man was demonstrating spectacular leg curls in an aerobics class, my crazy peeing-in-the-basin neighbour nudged me and with an impish wink asked, 'What do you reckon?'

Her words hung in the air, and I couldn't help but smile. There was something about the challenge, about the anticipation and game that thrilled me. I shot back, 'I reckon.'

An upcoming college fancy dress party provided the perfect opportunity to take matters into my own hands. I wanted to make sure I gave off the right signals, so I chose my appropriately trashy outfit carefully – a very short blue nurse outfit with white stockings and suspenders.

My latest target fittingly arrived as Batman. Although we both wanted to get it on hammer and tongs, we had to be careful. I hadn't seen it in writing, but the word was that college rules prohibited fraternising in each other's rooms. Each time we were near each other, the air seemed to crackle with the heady scent of lust, pulling us dangerously close to the edge of losing control. Every glance and every brush of skin felt like an invitation. We were teetering on the brink of something inevitable.

As the night came to an end, he leaned into me and whispered, 'Okay, Room 24 it is.'

Discretion and my room were a concept doomed to fail. The dorms were filled with fellow students and the corridor walls were thin. The student rooms were side-by-side and were mirrored opposite, running the full length of the dormitory hallway. I snuck back to my room as planned and was awaiting his, hopefully discreet, arrival. Far from restrained or cautious, my caped crusader thundered down the corridor like a horse – hopefully a stallion – in the home straight at the Grand National.

The superhero impression continued into the bedroom and heralded the start of a lively few weeks at college. We had sex whenever the opportunity arose. One morning, we took an opportunity in the padded cell area where control and restraint training was held. Later that day, I returned for a class and while restraining my pee partner in a training drill, I took great delight in whispering in her ear that she was lying face down on the precise spot where my bare arse had been a few short hours before, which resulted in her squealing like a pig and me screeching with laughter.

All good things must come to an end. Someone overheard Batman's arrival at my room the night of the fancy dress party and decided to grass me up. Before long, I was summoned to a superior's office to face – oh how lucky I was – the super critical, jaded teacher who skilfully extracted every ounce of truth from me. In a matter of moments, I was unceremoniously 'back squadded' from Prison College – local lingo for getting kicked the fuck out – for my indiscretions and transferred to another college to complete my training.

The new college was a world of misery. I joined a group of students who were already ten weeks into their training. They were a tight-knit unit that had zero interest in inviting this interloper into their gang. I was lonely and disillusioned and could but dream of all the fun my former fellow students were having while I sulked around a campus on the other side of the country.

Fortunately, my expulsion did not put off Batman, and we made a point of catching up with each other whenever he came to town. I last saw him by chance in late 2011 while attending a conference – ironically at the very college where I had been back squadded after news of our fling had become public. Lounging around the coffee machine during a break in sessions, I heard a familiar voice behind me. 'Room 24?'

I turned to find my superhero, still full of confidence and a very attractive specimen. He was as smooth as always, telling me I looked great and leaning over, whispered, 'How about one last romp, for old times' sake?'

I politely laughed off his offer. I had taken one small step towards being a real grown up and while I felt proud of myself, I also wondered if I had become a bit boring...

Looking back, the jaded teacher's judgement of me never becoming a governor stung. His words lit a fire within me. It pushed me to dig deeper and to prove to him – and more importantly to myself – that I was capable of achieving anything I put my mind to.

10

Dumb Dong the Bells are Gonna Shit

I found myself working in a place where the lines between danger and duty were blurred. I was navigating a world of hardened criminals, flirtations that crossed professional lines, and the constant reminder that every day could be my last. The mission for me wasn't just to survive, but to thrive and, let's be honest, I hadn't shown any green shoots that grew towards the latter to this point in my life.

My journey through Prison College was mostly enjoyable, which came as a surprise given my classroom credentials. It helped that there was the obligatory superhero fling, and a few likeminded peers who egged me on.

I remember most fondly the unfamiliar mental stimulation. It was the first time I had used my brain in a very long time and although a little rusty, it still worked!

That first year on the job taught me more than just the technicalities of my role – it ignited a deeper understanding of myself and revealed an inner drive I hadn't known existed. I learnt that I had the strength to push through difficulties while keeping my focus on the bigger picture, even when the obstacles felt insurmountable. However, the real turning point came when I discovered a new side of myself – an appetite for promotion and an unshakeable desire to move up the ranks faster than the traditional path would allow.

Patience had never been one of my virtues, and waiting five years to sit the senior officer exam felt like an eternity. I was determined to find a way to fast-track my career, with being a governor the final destination. It wasn't just about getting ahead for the sake of it, it was about proving to myself that I could. I made a vow to stop whinging about my work in the segregation unit and instead focus on what I could change to make my situation better. This shift in mindset sparked an all-consuming desire to get out of the female section and work with male prisoners, where I felt more comfortable and confident. And, if I'm being honest, I was scouting for a potential husband amongst the male prison officers.

The new year started well with the granting of my request for a transfer to the men's prison, and just as I had met Myra Hindley on my first day of a new posting, this time, I met a character of equal notoriety – John.

John exuded a magnetic presence as he lounged back in his big leather director's chair, muscles splashed with a medley of tattoos and bulging out of his shirt. He gave me a look that seemed to say, *Do as you are told on my watch and you will be fine,* which I found strangely attractive.

I was consumed by thoughts of John as my next conquest. 'He is mine,' I said as I marched to the toilet to fix my hair.

Even though my lust must have been obvious, John didn't seem to notice that I had a crush on him and it's fair to say that my attempts at saucing up my physical appearance and detouring around the office in the hope of bumping into him delivered few results. So, I resorted to Plan B.

'Tony,' I said to one of the friendly young officers who seemed to have a good rapport with John, 'do you think John knows how much I fancy him?'

Tony, ever the easy-going officer, seemed amused but not surprised. 'He's never said anything along those lines to me, but I'm happy to convey your feelings and let you know his reaction.'

We were now entering a waiting game, so I shifted my focus back to my career. My new twenty-or-so teammates were all men, and responsible for over two hundred basic regime prisoners. Some of these prisoners were locked up for twenty-three hours a day because they were unable to follow basic prison rules.

It was a newly built wing, with a newly formed team. Did I mention they were all men? Wink. Wink. Naturally, I wondered how they'd handle the young, overly confident newcomer in their midst. Sure enough, just a few days after my arrival, I found myself in solitary confinement. The incident started when a couple of my colleagues, in a move I chose to describe as 'team building', convinced me that I should spend some time in a cell to fully empathise with those I cared for. It was a while before I realised I'd been tricked, and as I lay, bored on the hard cell bed, I had a tiny glimpse into time behind a heavy metal cell door. I learnt how small and noisy it was, how little privacy there was with a window on the back wall that had no curtain, and a glass viewing panel in the door. But what started as a pleasurable experience quickly turned into a throw-up-in-mouth nightmare when I left the cell. The cell was cleaned by prisoners and not exactly of operating theatre standards, and the bed must have been liberally sprinkled with short and curlies left by some sex-starved young man. During my time lying there, they had fused with my crisp white shirt, where they stood curly, proud and plentiful. Despite vigorous brushing, the revolting little critters remained steadfast throughout the day. However, I believed that I had passed the test and I was on my way to becoming a bona fide member of the team who could handle whatever curveballs – or curlies – might be thrown my way.

My fabulous colleagues became increasingly protective of me in this unpredictable and dangerous environment, and in many ways became my extended family. Beneath the hard-external veneer, they were big softies who cared about my welfare and always had one protective eye on me wherever I went.

There was one incident burned into my memory that did manage to rattle me to the core. As I walked through the prison shortly before lock-up one evening, I passed by a cell just as its inmate, a chap named Barney, attempted to slip a heroin wrap between the bars. One inch long and neatly folded, the distinctive brown hue in the corners indicated where the illegal substance had permeated the paper. Barney gave me his best if-you-interfere-I-will-kill-you look just as I lashed out at his hand and knocked the package to the floor. I stamped my right foot on top of where it landed. A Mexican standoff ensued. He gave me the Category A hard core prisoner stare learnt from those prisoners who pose the highest risk to the community and must not, under any circumstances, escape from prison.

While Barney had not quite progressed to crimes that would see him serving life in prison, he did have a bountiful criminal record for one so young. He was still in his early twenties, and his violent history dated back to his early teen years when he was first jailed for aggravated assault. More recently and while serving his five-year term, he had used a sharpened pen to viciously stab an officer in the neck.

Barney was a well-groomed young man with a fashionable hair style and a ripped body that suggested he spent many hours in the gym. In the absence of knowing anything about him, and based solely on what he looked like, many would consider him a catch outside prison. His undeniable style shone through, even when confined to the bland grey prison wear. He polished his look with a chic pair of branded trainers, making him stand out in the prison environment. If I didn't know anything about him, Barney would have caught my eye in a nightclub.

In my newly reformed world, I was now the matador and he was the bull, and the customary red flag lay trapped under my foot. The bull snorted and kicked its hind legs as if preparing to gore me just as the lock-up alarm shrilled.

Barney knew what that alarm signalled – the wing would soon be awash with big burly officers, the gates would clang as they shut, and my foot would remain firmly on the wrap of heroin. He would be caught, charged and sentenced. He made one last futile demand that I remove my foot, but I stared back, shaking my head confidently as I knew the cavalry would soon arrive.

The maximum penalty the prison could unilaterally impose in those days was forty-two days and these were duly added to his sentence, which had been very close to completion. In his mind, that meant that his abstention from the sex provided by his wanton and slightly crazy girlfriend had been cruelly extended. His intimidating glares whenever we crossed paths left me feeling more than a little uncomfortable.

With a string of varied activities making up the prison officer tasks, I found solace in one of the more sedate duties – listening in on telephone calls between prisoners and visitors. Our job was to ensure that nothing illegal was being discussed. Most were typical family calls, of the chit-chat variety. Sometimes a bit of sexual innuendo was tossed in to brighten up the day and prompt a giggle.

I was looking forward to my next telephone shift, which provided a break from the in-your-face stuff that was often part of our daily rounds and duties. I settled into my padded chair and pulled on the tabletop to wheel myself up to the desk. I reached out, retrieved a set of headphones, and placed them over my ears. I sat listening intently while fidgeting with my pen and settled in for what was mostly a relaxing time.

My trained ears listened intently to an innocuous conversation between a prisoner and friend. As it ended, I flicked the button to hook into another conversation and froze at the sound of a familiar voice.

'You find out where she lives,' it hissed. 'I don't care who is in the house with her, you burn the fucking place down, you get me?'

The menacing anger in his tone shook me to the point where I left the office and galloped over to a vantage point from where I could see everyone in the prisoner telephone area. The voice, unmistakably belonged to Barney, and I instinctively knew I was the 'she' he had referred to. While nothing came of the threat, the personal nature of the episode was a sobering reminder of *Toto, I've a feeling we're not in Kansas anymore!*

Managing risk and adapting to circumstances were crucial aspects of the job, and I had to always have my wits about me. Back then, the general code among male prisoners was not to harm women – excluding those with mental health issues clouding their judgment, and of course, those who blamed you for adding extra time to their sentence!

Being female actually seemed to push me into a more prominent role, especially when muscle-bound tough guys were smashing up their cells. While my male colleagues were fantastic, there were certain high-tension, testosterone-fuelled incidents that called for something different – what was perceived as the softer, more empathic approach that a woman could bring to the table. I had an ability to connect and talk through a situation, rather than simply confront it. It wasn't that I lacked the toughness or authority to hold my own, but my communication skills – the 'gift of the gab', as I like to call it – were becoming my most valuable asset.

Embracing the unique strengths of being a woman in a male-dominated environment became a gamechanger for me. It wasn't about fitting in or proving myself – it was more about owning what set me apart, and using the differences to make the team stronger.

11

Shit Watch

How are you at taking advice? Me? Shit. I had this unfaltering ability to shrug off the wisdom of others. Once again, my upward mobility was about to collide with the smelly reality of being wrong.

As an ambitious prison officer now saddled with a mortgage after buying the council house I had previously rented, I was now officially 'working class'. My newfound upward mobility called for a celebration and along with my friend Kelly, I had booked a holiday to Tunisia. Kelly, like most of my friends, was a single parent with a daughter a year younger than James. Although two years' my junior, the parallels in our lives cemented a strong connection.

As always, the duty-free shopping precinct at Gatwick Airport Departures was a hive of activity, with passengers scrambling for a last-minute bargain. I chose to pass the time with my own cursory bit of browsing. Almost immediately, a Tag Heuer ladies' watch taking centre stage in the jewellery store window caught my eye. It flashed intermittently at me like a lighthouse in choppy North Sea waters. Its calling was immediate and the bond with my wrist was instant. I bought it without hesitation, rationalising that if it lasted for sixty years, the six hundred pounds it cost translated into just ten pounds per year, less than one pound per month and a paltry three pence per day.

'This is an absolute steal,' I announced to Kelly, as I admired it draped over my wrist and strode towards the flight gate strutting like a top model.

94

Not one for following conventions, I wore my new watch proudly on my right wrist, which was tilted at just the right angle for everyone to admire the beauty of this fine piece of Swiss craftsmanship. The fact that I had just spent most of my holiday spending money was of no concern, as I was confident that this latest adornment would only add to my charm that was already legendary...

Upon arrival in Tunisia, the travel authorities advised against young foreign women walking the streets alone, and in a moment of rare intelligence, Kelly and I heeded the advice. Confined to the men who worked in the hotel, we endured a bit of a drought on the sex front, but the remaining two of the mandatory three holiday boxes to be ticked – sunshine and alcohol – were there in abundance.

'Who needs men when you have a newly acquired boyfriend in Mr Heuer,' I joked with Kelly. 'He's sure to keep me starry-eyed and entertained.'

My new love became a permanent fixture on my wrist, a symbol I proudly displayed each day.

I returned to work willing a large flashing neon arrow to appear on my forehead that pointed to my wrist.

'Very nice new watch you have there,' fellow officer and resident know-it-all Ben commented as I wrapped my wrist at the optimum angle around a coffee cup in the staff canteen.

'You are a complete nutcase if you plan to wear that while on duty as it's bound to get damaged,' he added, reminding me that if I hadn't taken out personal insurance on the watch, all I would get back from the Prison Service was a puny thirty quid.

I had no money for insurance after butchering my bank account to buy it, but I briefly pondered Ben's advice before hitting back. 'Don't be so fucking dramatic, Ben,' I said with a flick of my hair. 'I'll be fine and so will the watch. There's no reason to worry about insurance or damage as the geniuses in Tag's research and development laboratory in Switzerland have thought of everything. This sapphire diamond-cut glass is bullet proof, so much so that if a nuclear bomb were to hit us right now, the only things left in its wake would be a handful of cockroaches *and* my Tag Heuer.'

I went on enthusiastically, as a small crowd had gathered, eager to lend support to Ben's counsel. Being a plonker, I naturally ignored them and their disapproving glances, sure they were just expressing their envy.

Anyone who wasn't envious had something wrong with them as far as I was concerned, like one young man named Stan, an inmate in the segregation unit – or 'seg', as it was called. Stan's world was surrounded by either violent criminals or the mentally impaired. Like the female seg where I spent my first year, the male seg inmates were considered to be at high risk of harm to themselves or others if they mixed with the general prison population. So, they were kept in near-perpetual isolation and allowed just thirty minutes each day in the exercise yard. Their volatility also meant that a team of three to six officers had to serve their meals at their cell doors.

Ordinarily, it was a three-person team, with one officer opening the door, the second officer wheeling the food trolley into the doorway and the third serving the meal. The first two then kept watch to make sure nothing unsavoury happened to the third officer. Prisoners prone to violence were instructed to stand against the far wall of their cells, as having them anywhere near the trolley invariably left the prison officers wearing the food. With these violent prisoners, the cell door was unlocked, the tray of food slid in fast, and the door locked again quickly.

Stan was known to be an arse, but not a violent arse that required him to stand at the back of his cell – more just a verbal arse. Relaxed and even a little cheery, I approached his cell door and unlocked it with my left hand while resting my right hand on the handle. I couldn't help stealing an admiring glance at my Tag watch.

'Good afternoon, Stan. How are you? Here's your...' I said on entering the cell.

Before I could complete the sentence, a naked prisoner, armed with a three-inch turd in each hand, charged towards me. Whether it was a six-inch poo he had meticulously cut in half or whether he had a gift for delivering shits in identical proportions, I didn't ask.

'Aaaaaaargh...' he screamed, screeching to a halt just inches from my face.

His cold, troubled eyes focused on mine as the foul smell of excrement filled the air. Suddenly, he lurched forward, grabbed my arms just below the elbow and began to slowly and purposefully drag his shit-crayons down both arms. The turd on the left arm was daubed from my elbow to fingertips. The one on the right arm stopped abruptly as it encountered and became inextricably entwined with my Tag Heuer.

It was over in a flash. Colleagues came from everywhere to jump to my aid, pushing me and the meal trolley aside and pulling his cell door shut. Stan gave a little chuckle followed by a broad smile, revealing a mouth of mostly missing teeth that resembled and subsequently ruined my beautiful childhood memory of Stonehenge.

Fixed to the floor like a marble statue, I could only mutter, 'Shit.' Slowly and deliberately, my focus shifted to my watch...

'Shit, fucking shit, you fucking shit fuck,' I yelled in despair. 'What the fuck was that?' This felon's turd had gone into every little nook and cranny of the once beautiful, shining stainless-steel mastery of my watch.

Reality took over. I scurried down the hallway to the healthcare section to confirm that my Hepatitis B shot was still current. Relieved to have at least cleared that hurdle, I made my way to the bathroom to clean up as best I could. The crap flowed off my arms and hands and into the sink bowl. It swirled around before disappearing with loud gurgles down the drain. And while the running water and soap did a good job of cleansing me from the totally shit experience, it was powerless to repeat its exorcism of the excrement lodged firmly in the intricate strap of my watch. 'You dirty little fucker,' I cursed as my anxiety levels rose.

I turned the tap to full throttle. Water flew everywhere, bounding off the stainless-steel sink and shooting up towards the ceiling before cascading down to a now-soaked floor. 'Get the fuck out,' I wailed as the water seemed intent on having the opposite effect and was blasting ever smaller pieces of shit into even tinier gaps in the strap.

Exhausted and overcome with grief, I finally conceded defeat, placed the watch in an evidence bag and returned to work. That evening at home, I placed the bag and its stinky contents in the laundry cupboard where it remained locked up, sweating and festering for days while I considered my cleaning options. As time passed and the separation from my beloved watch became unbearable, my thinking became increasingly lateral.

'What do people do when they're constipated and need to break down their shit?' I asked during a telephone conversation with my mother one evening.

'They use Cod Liver Oil,' she replied in a tone that embodied a practical mother.

In that eureka moment, I reasoned that if the disgusting fluid feared by just about every British child of my era could loosen stools inside you, it could bloody well get to work on loosening the shit in my watch. So, in an exercise reminiscent of an Ebola virus researcher, I gloved up and filled a large soup bowl with the vile oil before carefully opening the sealed bag and emptying its putrid contents into the last chance vessel. After a night of submersion, I approached the morning inspection with some trepidation.

'Oh yes, here we go,' I said in high spirits at the sight of a few oscillating turd particles floating about.

The progress continued the following morning with more particles being released and even more the following day. By the fourth morning, it seemed every shit-bit had flaked off and floated to the surface. Again donning my Ebola suit, I carefully removed the watch from the bowl, grabbed a spare toothbrush and vigorously applied the finishing touches before giving it a thorough antiseptic soaking.

'It's good to go,' I announced triumphantly while wondering why I so frequently chose to ignore good advice – the elderly Greek gentleman on the train to the airport had suggested opening the carriage window was not a clever idea. I opened it. Ben and my colleagues had encouraged me not to wear the watch to work. I wore it.

Before tossing the used toothbrush in the bin, I toyed with the idea of keeping it for the future use of visitors of the I-don't-really-like-you variety. Perhaps George, who despite having had plenty of my shit, still had room for a little more?

Despite the shitty happenings, my mind was still focused on John, and I had started to do whatever I could to present myself and thrust my very best foot forward. The stock standard black and white uniforms made the task difficult, but I found ways to pretty myself up, turning to fifty shades of eyeliner and a range of creative hairstyles that flirted with the strict prison officer policy that required all shoulder length and longer hair to be tied back.

Finally, after watching me swan about and being told by my colleague Tony – at my behest – that I fancied him, John asked me out.

No matter how much I wanted to carve my own path, I needed to accept that the wisdom of others held great value. Fighting against advice and stubbornly pushing through only set me back. It was time to listen, learn and recognise when to pause and reflect.

12

Tits and Tat

The first date with your true love is meant to be perfect, right? Mine was not the one I'd been fantasising about. Every inch of me screamed, 'Run!' Facepalm – I didn't.

We had arranged to meet at a nearby pub and with the office dress code banished, I went for broke. Being naturally slim back in my twenties, I looked fabulous for our first date – even if I do say so myself. I wore my sexiest black dress with its spandex boob tube top and a fitted bottom half that celebrated my every curve. My more-belt-than-skirt showcased almost every inch of my legs that were anchored in skyscraper pink stilettos.

I arrived early and stole a quick visit to the ladies to double-check that everything was where it should be to deliver maximum wow. Satisfied, I settled at the bar eagerly awaiting John's arrival. When he entered a few minutes late, he glanced around the room and on spotting me and my revealing outfit, displayed a definite that's-an-eleven-out-of-ten mouth-gaping expression. However, my facial expression was the opposite. My beating heart stalled as he approached me, and the visual assault came into sharp focus.

'What. The. Fuck?' I said through gritted teeth as the cowboy approached. 'Surely he can't be serious wearing that shite in public?'

My immediate thought was to feign a heart attack or perhaps a dizzy episode that required me to flee immediately. It was too late. He leant over and planted a kiss on my forehead before heading off to get a drink.

There was no diplomatic way to describe his dress sense. He had morphed from a hot man in uniform into Woody from the set of *Toy Story*. A red Reebok T-shirt under a tight-fitting American mid-west denim jacket. The embroidered horse and cart adorning his back gave way to stone-washed jeans rolled up at the ankles. Brown suede brogues completed the crime unfolding right before my eyes. I had never imagined wearing a balaclava on a date before, but on this occasion, I'd have gladly made an exception. It was beyond embarrassing to be seen with Woody when I was expecting Buzz Lightyear.

I should have called time on the relationship right then and there, but I concluded that, dress sense aside, he still had all the ingredients for a happy-ever-after. The body was in showroom condition, the face appealing and I knew he was hot in uniform. My thoughts on how I would take the initiative and sort out a new wardrobe were interrupted by his return.

We settled in for an afternoon of gazing into infinity and beyond... He removed the denim jacket to expose rippling arms and as each glass of wine emptied, I sensed my beer goggles kicking in and I started to imagine having sex with a cowboy. By late afternoon the lust for the cowboy had become so unbearable that I contemplated unleashing my pent-up tension and tearing off his offensive clothes. The chemistry between us relegated conversation to a distant second and we spent the afternoon engaging in lengthy kissing that put the Love Mountains to shame.

'It might cost a bit to get him fashionable,' I debriefed a friend on the phone later that evening. 'But it will be worth every penny as this is a fairy tale waiting to unfold.'

That was my first mistake. I had ignored the truth in the saying that a woman cannot change a man because she loves him – a man changes himself because he loves her. But I pushed ahead, eager to tick the husband box and live the 2.4 family dream.

I told John the next day at work that his fashion sense was not acceptable if we were going to date in daylight, so he would need to bid farewell to the cowboy clothing. He took it well and showed scant resistance, not even when the time came to enter his home carrying several large plastic garbage bags and set about trawling through his wardrobe. Out went the collection of Hawaiian shirts, the assortment of MC Hammer pants, the cowboy jackets and the V-neck T-shirts with embossed cartoon characters on the chest. The garbage bags at bursting point, I stood back to admire an evening's work that had transformed the clutter to a minimalist marvel of just a few bits of underwear, his gym clothes and his work uniform.

'This is just the start,' I warned as he looked up from the lengthy shopping list I planted in his palm. 'It all continues on the weekend with a clothes shopping date.'

Having disposed of Exhibit A – the large black plastic garbage bags – I set about creating a wardrobe of tasteful splendour. Plain round neck T-shirts replaced the Aztec-patterned V-necks, MC Hammer jeans made way for a modern fit and all loud and brash colours were traded for subtle hues. He looked good. I felt even better when a now snappy-looking John told me I was the one he had been waiting for all these years – so I was his happy-ever-after too!

Initially living apart but inseparable, we made a point of using most weekends for romantic escapes. A few blissful months into the relationship and cosying up at a local Chinese restaurant where a 'special' got you five dishes for a mere ten pounds, he seemed uncharacteristically nervous. He fiddled with the tablecloth as he clutched his beer, taking deep gulps. Maybe he was having second thoughts about the special on the menu, I pondered. He cleared his throat and in an untranslatable tone asked, 'Will you marry me?'

It was like watching a movie with your parents – you are comfortable and at ease until an unannounced and particularly raunchy sex scene fills the screen. You freeze, hold your breath and wait for it to pass. This was my *Wolf of Wall Street* opening scene with my folks sitting next to me on the sofa.

It was like an out of body experience that I had no control of when I said, 'Yes.' I was devoid of any real emotion but, at that moment, it felt like the rite of passage to my adulthood.

A few days later we decided to book a celebratory trip to the Caribbean, reserving a top-notch hotel overlooking an idyllic palm-fringed beach. One evening, while home alone and paging through the Caribbean brochure, dreaming of our holiday together, I got a midnight urge to be with him. Despite heavy snow falling outside, I drove the short distance to John's home on the other side of town, imagining how passionately surprised he would be to have a visit from his darling fiancée.

I glided through the slush and into his long driveway. I could see an unfamiliar car parked near the house, and as I drew closer, I saw the light on in his upstairs bedroom.

'You fucker,' I cursed as I slammed the car door and marched with clenched fists along the gravel path leading to his front door.

Making great effort to cover my rage, I knocked gently while pressing my ear to the glass in the hope of hearing the distinctive sounds of a mad rush to clear the evidence. But there was nothing – not even footsteps coming down to open the door. I was convinced I knew what lay on the other side, and I banged again, this time more forcefully. Again, there was no response, so I attacked the door with all the strength I could muster. I was mid-bash when the door swung open and I nearly landed a solid jab right on John's nose. He stood there, stunned, and rather than rushing to embrace me and revel in the surprise of my visit, he offered a startled, 'What on earth are you doing driving in this weather, and at this time of night?'

Struggling to maintain the look of a doting, unsuspecting lover, I replied, 'I missed you, so I decided to surprise you.'

His face drained of colour. 'Ah, Honey, that's adorable, but I'm really tired tonight,' he proffered.

That was the breaking point. My veneer of calmness shattered and I stormed past him and attempted to climb the stairs, but he blocked my path.

'What are you doing?' I demanded.

'Nothing,' he replied, his voice sounding confused.

'So, why can't I go upstairs? Is someone else here?' I persisted.

'No,' he shot back, before darting up the stairs and flinging the bedroom door open while loudly announcing as he spread his arms, 'see, there is no one here!'

The picture of innocence lacked only a bunch of flowers held out to cover what I was convinced was deceit. I scanned the room for any tell-tale signs but there were none. I peered under the bed and behind the curtains. The room was empty, but my instinct told me there was a woman hiding somewhere.

'You can't fool me that easily, John. Who is she?' I quizzed angrily.

He chose to remain silent while I turned and stomped back down the stairs. He was right behind me, breathing down my neck in his eagerness to usher me from his home and retain his innocence. My head was now a tempest of angry thoughts, and I actually felt embarrassed for a moment that I was making such a scene when I had no real evidence to confirm my suspicions.

Then it hit me, I hadn't checked the wardrobe. I spun on the bottom step to dash back up and dodged past John, but somehow I got tangled up under his legs and I tripped and slipped back down the stairs. My curvaceous boobs impressively thumped on alternate steps, somewhat cushioning the ride.

I managed to charge back up the stairs again. This time, I reached for the wooden bannister to assist with the rapid ascent, but I knocked him off his axis and as he wobbled he grabbed one of my ankles to prevent himself falling backwards. Hanging taut mid-air between the two anchor points of my ankle and the bannister, like some poor soul on a medieval torture rack, our inadvertent tug-of-war ended – this time, the bannister railing came with me as it noisily broke free from the screws fixing it to the wall.

Fear swept over his face as he stared at me – an apparition of determination in a Fatima Whitbread pose, holding a makeshift javelin in my hands, surely poised to spear him and his possibly philandering genitals to the back wall.

Instead, I made a sudden and unexpected peace offering. 'This is juvenile, John. Let's just go back to my house and talk things through like civilised adults?'

He agreed, looking both relieved and a little suspicious.

His house was now dark and eerily silent. I took charge of locking up, pocketing both his house keys and his car keys before settling into my car for the journey home. As I reversed out of his driveway, I glanced up at the now-dark bedroom window, half expecting to see a guilty face at the window.

We drove in silence, neither of us quite sure what to say or how to discuss my Oscar-winning performance of the evening. Then I spotted the roadside verge I'd been looking for. I swerved in and hit the brakes hard, bringing the car to a screeching halt.

'And now?' he asked.

I opened my door, pulled his house and car keys from my pocket and hurled them over a cavernous ditch and into the pitch-black countryside, where the snow lay a foot deep.

'What the fuck are you doing?' he yelled in disbelief.

'Time for you to "jog on",' I snapped back. 'And here's three tips to help you on your way: Don't drink yellow snow if you get thirsty motherfucker, walk on the right side of the road and... have fun with your invisible woman as the engagement is off!'

With him barely out of the car, I floored the accelerator, sending slush with such force that it soaked him from head to toe. I glanced back just long enough to see my former wolf howling at the moon. Ahead of him lay a long, cold and dark trudge home.

The next day brought a new challenge – what to do about the Caribbean holiday? I wasn't about to cancel, choosing instead to call one of the hotties I met in Shagaluf. His name was Chris and he eagerly accepted the invitation to a free vacation. I was sure he was more excited about the fully paid week in the Dominican Republic than he was about me, but I couldn't have cared less. It was all about telling John I had found a new travelling companion, hoping to spark a jealous reaction that would prove conclusively that he really did love me.

Chris and I role-played as a couple throughout the trip, holding hands through the airport, cuddling on the plane and even at the hotel check-in. I had always been drawn to him, especially because he had this perpetual take-it-or-leave-it attitude with me. I should have felt wonderful about securing the company of this gorgeous and successful man, having him all to myself for an entire week in an exotic, sun-kissed paradise. But I didn't. Even his many stellar performances in the sack couldn't turn a good time into a great one.

The substitute trip did nothing to quench my competitive thirst. Yes, we had plenty of fun, but I thought about John often, fighting continuously with an ego that kept reminding me that this was one game I was not going to lose. I remained hungry to win, and I knew my only path to victory was to get back with my likely-a-cheat former fiancé.

My empty house looked particularly forlorn when I returned, and my sadness deepened to a level I had seldom experienced. I sat at home waiting for the phone to ring, imagining John's remorseful voice begging for forgiveness. But it never came.

It ended up being me who reached for the phone.

'I am sorry, John, I love you,' I sobbed pitifully when he picked up the receiver. 'I had a terrible time away. I couldn't stop thinking about you and I want you back. Please forgive me. Let's start afresh and never mention Cupboardgate or the Caribbean holiday again,' I added.

Engagement Mark II was officially launched with a clear takeout message: tit for tat... or something equally life stupid.

My desperation to be married and live happily ever after meant I ignored the signs. The truth is, if you must wonder whether someone truly loves you, they don't. The end was already written, but the fuckwit in me chose not to read the large flashing fluorescent sign right in front of my face.

13

You fat Cunt

By now you would realise I'm the type who when told building a
sandcastle on quicksand is not going to end well, I grab the metaphorical
bucket and spade and give it a shot anyway. I'd been riding high on
my delusions of happily ever after, convinced that if I kept building, I'd
eventually get a castle. Unsurprising spoiler alert: I didn't!

My ill-advised efforts to rebuild shattered trust convinced me that life
was once again rosy. Two short months after Cupboardgate and the
Caribbean fling, John and I moved in together in my Chalkstone estate
home. We both had good jobs, so our spare cash gave us a materialistic life
I'd not experienced before. A now eleven-year-old James bonded with his
sporty new stepdad-to-be. They spent many hours together, connecting
through a mutual love of football. I dared to dream that we would live
happily ever after despite knowing that the foundations were built on
sand. Our seemingly happy and normal life was a façade, but I pushed on
creating an illusion in my own circus.

Our wedding date was booked and fast approaching but I still found
time for the occasional catch up with Batman from Prison College. I'd
get a random call, asking me if I wanted to be 'Batman's Knobbin', which
I found irresistible every time. Why I believed everything would be
perfect once John and I were married was staggeringly irrational. Our
already troubled relationship destabilised further as I received one work
promotion after another, resulting in more and more hours away from

home. There was no congratulatory acknowledgement from him, never a sign that he was happy for me.

The people around us must have picked up on our unhappy signals and I began to fear that no one would attend our wedding. I needed a solution, and quickly.

'Honey, why don't we do something exotic for our wedding and marry in a tropical location?' I suggested one night over dinner. 'Just the two of us and James, what do you say?'

He didn't seem particularly interested, as he stuffed another piece of steak in his mouth, but he let out a gruff sound that I took to be a yes. I got onto it immediately, searching the internet for options. Eventually, I settled on a particularly upmarket venue in the Caribbean favoured by Westerners. The resort looked perfect and promised that we would feel 'the pulse of paradise' the moment we arrived.

My attention then turned to the big day when no expense would be spared. I learnt that the resort had an ornate old-world carriage for hire for romantic occasions. Drawn by a team of stately white horses, its red velvet seats added to a fairy-tale picture. Carriage booked, I found and engaged a local wedding celebrant, arranged an appointment at the resort's hair salon and reserved a table in Barbados's most lavish restaurant for our reception dinner.

All planned with military precision, we flew out a few days ahead of my big box-ticking moment, confident that everything would be perfect. Alarm bells rang but were customarily ignored as we traipsed around in our trademark distant manner. Mere days away from our nuptials, I continued to brush aside the huge, illuminated sign which said, *Don't Do It!*

With just hours to go until I was to be married, I shuffled uncomfortably in the hair salon chair. As my lengthy appointment came to a glorious end, my gaze fell on the vast mirror in front of me. The new hairstyle was gorgeous, but it couldn't mask the anguished face staring back at me.

'Who are you? And where are you going with this?' the face whispered. In that split second, neither the reflection looking back at me, or I, had the answer.

Doubt assaulted me from every direction. I still had no answer a few hours later when, looking fabulous in an expensive designer wedding dress, I sat like royalty in my horse-drawn carriage. It rumbled along the narrow, cobbled street, carrying me to an awaiting red carpet that inched its way into a quaint beach chapel. Inside, John, James, and the local preacher awaited me, accompanied by a pair of inebriated British holidaymakers happily hauled off the beach to act as witnesses. I squinted my eyes in the late afternoon sun trying to get a better view of the whitewashed chapel – and perhaps even catch a glimpse of the not-my-happy-ever-after man I was about to marry. He would be inside waiting for me at the altar. I knew he would be sweating, probably wondering what the hell he was doing marrying *me*!

'What the fuck am I doing?' I mumbled.

Sensible people might have jumped from the carriage and done a runner, but I reasoned that having a husband had always been a key item on my life's checklist, and I was a heartbeat away from achieving that goal. Our chosen wedding song was 'Runaway' by The Corrs, and the irony of the lyrics wasn't lost on me as I walked down the red carpet towards the altar – *I would run away, yeah, yeah. I would run away.*

As the thought of running away crossed my mind, my alter ego seemed to take over. I found myself blurting out, 'I do,' in response to the all-important question – even though I knew deep down I didn't. I told myself that maybe this was how everyone felt at the altar. Perhaps the stuff of happily-ever-after was meant for fairy tales and make-believe, not for real life...

The evening celebration meal was little better, with tears the fitting theme. My mother wept when I called her back in the UK to announce that John and I had just got married. She regained her composure long enough to chastise me and tell me that I remained a 'silly, silly girl'.

As we settled into married life, our relationship slowly eroded who I thought I was. I had forgotten how to laugh. Being myself seemed to make matters worse, so I stopped and lost all the things about myself that I enjoyed. We would quite literally go for months without speaking, even though we shared a car for our long commute each day. Predictably, I allowed my work to consume me, putting all my energy into it and avoiding going home as much as I could.

A huge realisation hit me one day while meeting some of the new prison officer recruits. A sassy young lady bounced into the room, reminding me of who I used to be just a few years earlier. Attitude and swagger oozed from her as she faced me – her new boss. She stood towering in the doorway, a former beautician and an absolute stunner. Every curve shone through her top-to-toe body-hugging black motorcycle leathers, which would have had Max of poxy puffer jacket fame eating his heart out. But her striking poise and smile vanished as she extended her hand to introduce herself. For a moment she stalled, stammering a little as if searching for the right words. Then, in a moment of vulnerability, she just let the truth flow. 'Please be nice to me. I really need this job.'

Shaken by her brutal honesty and genuine apprehension, I held her stare and simply replied, 'I got you, sister.'

The ninety-plus hours I worked each week to escape the harsh reality of my unhappy marriage only increased my stress, and I began experiencing frequent episodes of sleepwalking. Ironically, amid this exhausting cycle, it provided me with a way to release a bit of stress without facing any immediate consequences. My sleepwalking and sleep talking became an almost nightly occurrence. The most memorable episode played out one evening as we were both drifting off to sleep. I turned over in bed with my arms extended in a dramatic flailing motion. Without realising it, I delivered a sharp backhanded slap right between John's eyes. He woke me up, told me what I'd done, and I offered an insincere apology more out of habit than actual regret. The next day, I couldn't help but smile, wondering just how much I must dislike him to do that in my sleep. Then, I paused and reflected on how my subconscious was clearly sending me a loud message, one I was choosing to ignore, at least for a little bit longer.

One evening, while relaxing on the sofa watching the *Jerry Springer Show*, I saw contestants piercing the strangest parts of their bodies. Eyelids, ears, noses and lips were old news, so, each contestant pushed the limits to impress the audience. It was strange, but for the first time in as long as I could remember, I found myself laughing. Maybe the weirdness of the show reflected the state of my life – painful, just like the contestants' bodies?

I could do that, I thought. *I'll have my vagina pierced!*

I laughed at the idea at first, quickly dismissing it as ridiculous. But the bored housewife in me couldn't shake the feeling that I needed to do something spontaneous. I eventually settled on the idea of inserting a small nut and bolt contraption into my clitoris hood, *yup*, made perfect sense at the time...

I should have known things wouldn't end well when I walked into a piercing studio that doubled as a shabby tattoo parlour. The owner did nothing to calm my growing unease. He emerged from behind a curtained area, his excessively tight leather trousers accentuating his crown jewels. With a strange mix of Rod Stewart's body and Jimmy Savile's face, he led me to a cabinet displaying various piercing options.

With a vulgar grin at my stainless-steel ball and bolt selection, he said, 'You will need to get your gear off love, everything from the waist down.'

Patting a stool-like armless chair to summon me, the confident mullet-man slathered, 'Right, jump up here, let's get to work on you.'

He grabbed his Sweeney Todd looking implements and slipped on his latex gloves, snapping them in a scene reminiscent of Dr Frank N Furter in the *Rocky Horror Picture Show*. Down on his knees, he was up close and personal with my smashed crab and seemed to be enjoying every prod and dig as he applied the anaesthetising gel. I looked up at a grubby and water-stained ceiling as he started to fiddle, praying that he was a skilled operator and would not deviate from the agreed procedure. Fifteen minutes later, he gave the nut and bolt a little flick, stood back to admire his work and flashed a wink in my direction.

'Perfect! Job looks great, and it's not goin' nowhere,' he declared as I reached for my gear and redressed myself at the speed of light.

A week or two later at work and busting for a piddle, I rushed to the loo to discover that the little head nut from the bolt had vanished and was – judging by the upward and uncontrollable piss fountain – up my pee hole. I finished my business, wiped down the seat and the floor and dashed to inform my trusted work girlfriend.

'My piercing has come loose and there's a part of it swimming around inside me, at least I think there is,' I blurted out in an anguished voice.

'What's the fuss,' she replied while trying not to laugh. 'Just go back to the tattoo parlour and get Bondage Bill to whip it out.'

We caught up again over the lunch break, where again she delighted in suggesting that the only solution to my vexatious vaginal conundrum was a return visit to the tattoo parlour. I couldn't bear another embarrassing visit to the GP after the pregnancy and acid-derived gerbil episodes. Besides, what would I tell the doctor when he asked what my ailment was?

'It's like this, doctor, I have this little stainless-steel ball up in my piss-pipe...' Yeah, right! There was no frigging way I would put myself through that humiliation. I reasoned that my dignity would take less of a bashing at Rod Stewart forward-slash Jimmy Savile's joint. A return to the seedy villain who created the problem in the first place – keeping no record of the transaction – definitely trumped a doctor whose profession demanded he record in my file that he had to correct a genital piercing for the fuckwit patient whose life was like watching a train crash.

Bondage Bill seemed genuinely happy to see me and engaged in a bit of grubby sexual innuendo before again popping me onto the stool. Naked from the waist down and legs spreadeagled, the sleazebag massaged the missing piece from a pipe that hid a whole lot of I didn't know what.

With all the skill of an acne-inflicted youngster squeezing a massive spot, he slowly coaxed it out while making a series of unsettling noises more suited to enticing a kitten from the top branches of a tree. I was distraught that this stainless-steel contraption had become a metaphor for a life in a mess. It signified a person who had rattled along down the wrong path and had got lost down a hole...

After leaving Bondage Bill's parlour, I made my way to the nearest coffee shop. Sipping a soothing café latte, I took a moment to reflect. I questioned my contribution to our marriage and life in general. Had I been a good wife, or my rash old self? There was no clear answer. It felt like we had both failed each other to lesser or greater degrees; his version, my version, and the truth likely somewhere in between. With the word 'failure' screaming from the rooftops, I left the coffee shop weighed down by regret.

Stepping into the crisp spring evening, the air thick with the scent of fresh buds and the promise of better days, it hit me. Maybe it was time for a fresh start. A change of scenery; a chance to clear our heads before we made any hasty decisions about our future together. Life could skip along and I could pretend the inevitable wasn't looming just around the corner.

The call of fate, or perhaps fate's slightly more awkward cousin, arrived on what would have been just another day at work. My colleague approached, waving a copy of *The Sun* newspaper like a flag of impending doom.

'We need to talk. Now!' she hissed – a sentence no one ever wants to hear. 'Follow me... to the toilet.'

With a shared look of silent panic, we marched purposefully towards the ladies' room. She slammed the door behind us, shoved the tabloid in my face, and spat, 'What the actual fuck? You're plastered across page seven in the fucking *Sun* newspaper!'

I wished she was wrong. But she wasn't. That one night in Majorca – a brief rendezvous with a celebrity, remember the one who had just split from another celebrity – had ended with a photographer's sneaky click.

And now that photo was splashed across the UK's largest selling national paper. With no hint of shame, some paparazzi had taken the liberty of sharing it with the entire world.

I could feel the blood drain from my face. 'What the hell do I do now?' I pleaded.

With a sweaty palm, I grabbed the offending newspaper and walked to the Governor's office. I knocked on her door – not with the confidence of someone facing their boss, but with the trepidation of a teenager who'd just been caught sneaking out their bedroom window.

Her husky voice called me in, and I sheepishly handed her the page. She leaned back in her leather chair, lit a cigarette like she was in some 1970s noir film, and took a slow drag. 'Is this the worst of it?' she asked, blowing a smoke ring casually.

I had no clue if it was the worst of it. It was Club 18-30. Years ago. There could be pictures of us on a beach or, God forbid, doing something even worse. But I wasn't about to get into it. I just nodded and said, 'Yes, Governor.'

She exhaled, casually flicked the page into the bin, and said, 'Alright, back to work then.' After a short pause, she added, 'I like you more now. You are a little on the wild side, aren't you?'

I froze, unsure if I should be thrilled or terrified. Was this some sort of compliment or a veiled threat? 'Uh, thanks Governor,' I muttered, then quickly made my escape.

John, as you can probably imagine, was less impressed about his wife filling the headline, and I tried to figure out how to apologise for something that was clearly not my fault and had happened many years before I met him.

I thought maybe a change of scenery could get John and I over this hump in the road. My parents had recently moved to Cyprus and with Mum's sixtieth birthday fast approaching, I had a brainwave. A family trip to the eastern Mediterranean. The perfect antidote to all our woes. And maybe, just maybe, a chance to reset.

CLAIRE PARKINSON

Soon after we landed in Nicosia, a couple of days before Mum's birthday, we slipped back into our characteristic silence, where we remained cocooned in misery for the entire week of the trip.

My mother's patience, already stretched thin, finally snapped on her birthday. We had packed a delicious picnic lunch, complete with birthday cake and sixty candles ready for a carefree day at a local water park. The plan was to spend the day frolicking in the water, tackling slides and chatting beneath the shade of a large umbrella reserved just for our family. But John opted out, choosing instead to remain isolated with his beach towel on the far side of the pool area.

'What the hell is going on?' Mum finally exploded, her frustration spilling over.

I didn't answer. I didn't need to – she could already read the look on my face. She knew I had mentally checked out.

Our final days on the island were spent on the beach where, despite the beautiful surroundings, we were encased in an impenetrable silence. Desperate to break the tension, I tossed a few grains of sand in John's direction, a futile attempt to spark some conversation, if only for my parents' sake.

'Care to join me for a swim?' I asked, my voice tinged with both hope and resignation.

He struggled to show any enthusiasm – people have walked to the gallows with a greater spring in their step. But begrudgingly, he did drag himself into the water where I tried to lighten the mood by playfully splashing him with water. He muttered something in response to my joviality, but his words were so quiet, I couldn't make them out. Still, the fact that we were at least speaking was encouraging.

'Sorry? I didn't quite catch that,' I asked, leaning in a little.

He lifted his gaze from the crashing waves, turned to me and met my eyes. He stared for a moment, as if deciding whether to speak. Then slowly and deliberately, mimed something to me. I had no real clue what he was trying to say. By that point, my confirmation bias on all things

John had reached such a level that I interpreted his lip movements as saying, 'Fat cunt.'

I'd been called a cunt a lot in the prison environment, and in the spirit of friendly banter, it usually didn't bother me. But the combination of 'fat' and 'cunt' sent me into a predictable spin. I took a deep breath, trying to suppress the sting of any reference to my weight. For a split second, I wondered if I had misread his lips but quickly concluded it didn't matter. Whether he said it or not, that was the moment – the straw that broke the camel's back. I had been waiting for a tipping point – a moment that would push me to finally plan my exit from this marriage – and now, it had arrived. I said nothing. I finished my swim in silence, my mind racing as I processed my next steps.

When my thoughts finally settled in some semblance of order, I left the water and walked over to where Dad was sitting on the beach.

'Dad, I'm going to divorce John,' I said, my voice steady but heavy with resolve.

A flicker of happiness crossed his face, almost identical to the look he had given me on the lawns of Wandlebury when I announced I was leaving Max. Just like then, he reached out, wrapped his arm around my shoulder and pulled me close.

'That's wise and it makes me happy,' he said, emphasising 'wise' as though he had just witnessed an epiphany. 'So, what now?' he asked, his voice gentle but curious.

'I'm going to divorce John, apply for another job, sell our house and buy myself and James a new home – in that order,' I replied, feeling a weight lift as the plan began to take shape.

I would tell John my decision when I was ready – when the time felt right.

Back in the UK, I didn't allow myself to admit that I was neurologically unwell. At the time, I convinced myself my symptoms were just stress-related – a diagnosis I'd obtained from visiting Dr Google. My drive to escape my financially constrained past refused to let me take time off to recover. I pushed through, working punishing hours while secretly planning for a new life. But as the days wore on and my symptoms worsened, I reluctantly acknowledged that I needed to see a professional. So, I made an appointment to see a neurologist, knowing deep down that I could no longer ignore the warning signs.

A new job was still my priority. I'd applied for a promotion and made the shortlist. The most enticing part of it being that the position was in another part of the country. The move would not only mean a new home but thrust me into a completely new world – one where no remnants of my soon-to-be ex would linger. I would be far enough away to pretend the past six years had never happened.

On the day of my final interview, I carefully selected a pair of masculine black pinstripe trousers, a starched white shirt and a black tie. I wanted to leave no doubt in the minds of those considering my application that I was more than capable of excelling in a male-dominated work environment.

Humour once again helped me break the ice just as it had at my Hank interview a few years earlier, and the two gentlemen sitting across from me chuckled at my responses. The younger of the two seemed particularly eager to hire me, a suspicion confirmed as I left the room. 'Well, if you don't hire her, I will,' he said to his offsider, loud enough for me to hear.

Riding high from the interview, I rushed straight to a follow-up appointment with the neurologist to finally get some answers about my symptoms. A week earlier, he had suspected a facial palsy but needed further tests to confirm his diagnosis.

'Welcome back,' he said, in a grave tone. 'Your results have come back and I'm afraid you are quite unwell. There is no easy way of saying this. You have a chronic neurological disease for which there is no cure. But you can help yourself and reduce the impact of the disease by effectively managing the stresses in your life.'

He continued talking but I couldn't concentrate on what he was saying. My head spun. My entire world had just been turned upside down.

'Fuck, fuck and fuck again,' echoed through my mind as I drove the sixteen-or-so miles home, lost in thought. 'This will not define me but it sure as hell will drive a better future for me,' I confirmed over and over.

I realised that if John and I didn't communicate when I was fit and healthy and had so much to talk about, what would it be like if I were confined to home and unable to communicate at all? The thought struck me like a bolt of lightning, and I was finally awake. On instinct, I reached for my Kelly Clarkson CD from the glove compartment and shoved it into the car's console. *Because of You* filled the car, and I sang along with what I will insist was perfect harmony, the music providing a valuable moment of comfort. The words, the melody, the release – it felt like I was singing my way out of the darkness, one note at a time.

The time had come. Knowing what had to be done, I marched boldly into the house, my heart pounding in my chest. I found John at the kitchen sink, his back to me as he washed the dishes. My adrenaline surged and my hands trembled with the weight of what I was about to say.

'I want a divorce,' I said, my voice flat, almost robot-like. No room for hesitation.

He paused, his hands still damp as he dried them slowly, his movements deliberate. Then he turned to face me, his expression soft as if he knew I'd just received bad news about my health.

'Please don't,' he said gently, his voice quiet but earnest.

In that moment, I saw it in his eyes – the unspoken truth. He knew his words were wasted, that my mind was made up. This was the end. There was no turning back.

'I have to apply my own oxygen mask before I can help anyone else. My health has to come first,' I replied, my voice steady. I extended my hand in a gesture of friendship.

'I don't want to be your fucking friend, I want to be your fucking husband,' he shot back, his frustration with me clear.

Maybe he was right, and I was being insensitive. But in my eyes, that was the problem. Whether it was my fault, his, or both of ours, from the beginning to the end, we had never been friends. He was a good man, just not the right man for me.

There was nothing solid beneath the surface of a shallow love – no foundation of trust, laughter or friendship. It was simply an existence alongside one another, coasting on the hope that things might get better – that somehow the cracks would heal themselves – they didn't.

14

Goodubai Guy

You know how some people emerge from the wreckage of a broken relationship with dignity and a renewed sense of purpose? Yeah, that wasn't me. My journey back to single lady status was a clusterfuck, the likes of which should only be confessed to a therapist after summoning the courage to admit it. But hey, if you're going to crash and burn, you might as well do it in a sparkly new outfit, with a glass of champagne in hand, right?

Within a day, I could already feel the obligatory divorce diet kicking in, and I started to feel more like myself than I had in a very long time. I treated myself to a hair make-over, a spray tan and a new wardrobe. Yes, it was the official launch of my very public early-onset mid-life crisis. After six painfully slow years of marriage, I was attracting attention again – and honestly, I was loving it. My mojo? Back in full force.

We continued living under the same roof for about a month, but the strain was unbearable. John wisely agreed to move out. I had an occasional moment of jealously when thinking about him moving on. But I forced myself to acknowledge the ridiculousness of such a notion and instead focused on a guy from my local gym who had a really nice bum. The bum belonged to a gorgeous young man named Greg, and his interest in me was the perfect escape from the reality of divorce. Thoughts of John with another woman quickly got relegated to the who-fucking-cares pile, and Greg and I embarked on a whirlwind romance. Great sex?

Absolutely. Weekend getaways in fancy hotels? Tick. Visits to wildlife parks? Tick. Dinners at classy restaurants? Tick. He even left sweet notes on the bathroom mirror, written with his finger in the steam, *Morning, beautiful.*

Part of me was enchanted by the dreamy attention Greg showered on me. For a moment, I let myself imagine that maybe, just maybe, this thing could last more than a month. But deep down, I knew he was just my rebound, and his life was more suited to a Walter Mitty fantasy than anything real. He claimed to own a house on a country estate, complete with horses. The truth? He lived in a small room on the estate and cleaned horse stables to cover his rent. Predictably, I grew tired of his tall tales and decided to let him live his fake life without me.

It was during a workday, standing next to a male colleague almost ten years my junior, that I saw the perfect opportunity to talk about excerpts I'd heard about from the book: *Men are from Mars, Women are from Venus.* I'd worked with this chap for a couple of years, and knew he was solid and our conversation would remain just between us.

'Do you think there is such a thing as happy ever after?' I asked casually.

'Yes, I think so,' he replied, raising an eyebrow.

'Oh, you *think* so... that sounds like a conversation over a glass of wine is required?' I shot back, fishing.

'Maybe it is,' he added.

We both paused. An awkwardly long pause. In that weird, moment, the spark between me and the man who would become my Lucky Number Three (LNT) was lit.

As I left the building that evening, I saw LNT for the first time in a different light – actually, quite sexy. It was one of those moments when you feel someone's eyes on you and wonder whether they're looking at your bum as you leave the room. I spun round, and there he was – eyes locked on me, contemplating, maybe for the first time, the woman he had just connected with. While I wasn't technically his boss, I was now one of the governors in this huge London prison, so being his superior, this was new and exciting territory.

LNT was in his mid-twenties, with short black hair, brown eyes and a muscular build. He played a lot of rugby and while a gentle soul off the field, he was a force to be reckoned with on it. Though his looks might've belonged to a self-assured guy, he lacked confidence around women. Modest, humble, and intriguingly shy – was he the perfect choice?

By this time, my three-fold commitment to my father in Cyprus was well underway. I had filed for divorce, applied for and won a promotion, and was preparing to put the marital home we had shared on the market.

I dreamed of a fourth wish, the cherry on the top – my happily ever after. It suddenly felt within reach as I began organising my farewell party from my big city prison job as 2005 was coming to an end.

'I'm having a leaving party next Wednesday,' I blurted to LNT, while doing my governor rounds one morning. Before he had time to digest my statement, I added, 'You're picking me up and taking me to the pub.'

'No problem, tell me where and when,' he replied. True to his word, he was there.

With the hope of starting 2006 with a bang, LNT ended up joining me at a friend's house, where we shared a disastrous night of sex. In hindsight, it was a hasty decision, fuelled by too much alcohol to have any semblance of a meaningful encounter. If I'm honest, my motivation wasn't exactly noble; I was determined that Walter Mitty wouldn't be my last sexual encounter of 2005...

The next morning, we drove to work in near silence, both of us trying to process what had happened the night before. Before we exchanged an awkward goodbye, and despite the tension, we somehow managed to agree on a dinner date a few nights later.

Sitting in front of a crackling fire eating fish and chips at an old country pub, I couldn't help but appreciate the peacefulness of the moment. There was something satisfyingly normal about it. I realised that LNT could be a stabiliser after the chaos of my past. I had kissed too many frogs, and it suddenly dawned on me that my true prince might just be a quiet and unassuming man. But I needed to be sure... Clearly, wisdom still eluded me.

I decided to cast the net a little wider than the familiar confines of the Prison Service in search of a comparator group to benchmark LNT against. Fresh from a long-term relationship, I was firmly in miserable o'clock remission and determined to improve my odds for a winning future. Online dating seemed like the perfect solution. I could browse endless profiles without worrying about who they really were. So, I prepared my profile and within seconds of posting it, I was hit by a tsunami of likes and winks from men who, like me, had heard the rumour that there's someone out there for everyone.

Among the crowd was a man who seemed promising – handsome, working in a gym, with a physique to match. His profile read well, and he could actually spell, which earned him enough kudos to warrant a date. With time of the essence, it was just a day later that I found myself sitting in a small country pub awaiting 'gym guy'. He walked in and I recognised him from his profile picture immediately. He spotted me and purposefully strode towards my table. He certainly was a handsome fellow, but there was not a lot of him – five-foot-fuck-all at best. He was another character straight from the movies! Lord Farquaad, the little villain from *Shrek*, had just entered my life. Gym guy took his tiny steps towards me, moving ever closer to an uncomfortable moment when I would need to make a tricky decision. Should I stand up to greet him even if my lofty stature might make him feel self-conscious? I chose to remain seated. His facial expression when I stayed put suggested he found my decision a bit weird. We survived an uncomfortable date and went our separate ways just one awkward hour later.

My next hit was marginally more successful, this time jagging a date with a sophisticated fellow. He worked in Dubai in some high-flying job and was clearly loaded. Fair-haired, blue-eyed and of average build, I struggled to get past his uncanny resemblance to Max. Disconcerting though it was, conversation flowed easily enough for us to agree to a follow-up date at a chic new city restaurant. He was perfect in so many ways, but the spark was utterly absent for me. I doubt even plugging him into the wall would have generated electricity between us.

The year was quickly winding down, and I promised myself that before it was time to belt out *Auld Lang Syne*, I would decide whether rich Dubai Guy or not-so-rich LNT would be ringing in the new year with me.

I had arranged to see Dubai Guy on Christmas Eve morning and LNT that evening – an admittedly obnoxious move to compare the two. The meticulously punctual Dubai Guy arrived exactly on time, knocking gently on the front door, his arms laden with expensive gifts. One of them was a beautiful Mont Blanc pen with a large sapphire solitaire on the lid. I thanked him profusely but coolly. We had lunch in a cosy Oxford restaurant, but the conversation was stiff and uncomfortable, signaling the inevitable end of our time together. Dubai Guy sensed it too and with an obligatory Christmas peck on the cheek and the briefest of soft hugs, we bade each other an impassive farewell.

The contrast with LNT's arrival an hour later was nothing short of galactic. I felt a quickening of my pulse and lightness in my head as I sat impatiently on the sofa, doodling with my Mont Blanc pen awaiting his arrival. When he arrived, he felt more like an old friend. Despite being empty-handed, he carried enough electricity to light up a metropolis and I instantly sensed something special between us. We spent the rest of the evening eating chocolate and watching TV, the only mildly uncomfortable moment arising when he pointed to my gift lying on top of its Christmas wrapping.

'What's this?' he asked unsuspectingly as he stretched over to retrieve it.

'That's a Mont Blanc pen,' I explained in a less than convincing attempt at nonchalance. 'It has a sapphire in it,' I continued while his puzzled look suggested he couldn't quite compute how anyone would wish to spend thousands of pounds on a pen when a ten pence Bic did the job just fine.

'Wow, so who gave you that?' he asked.

Normally quick on my feet, I nearly tripped over my own words. I wasn't about to tell him about Dubai Guy, at least not then as it might have put a dent in what was shaping up to be a perfect Christmas Eve. I stumbled and stuttered as my brain scrambled to concoct a believable white lie.

'The girls at work clubbed together to buy it for me,' was the best I could produce.

LNT clearly saw though it but smiled and said nothing, leaving me in a momentary quandary – here I was telling a white lie to someone I may actually spend the rest of my life with.

There was no Saint Christopher medallion flying through the air, no bevy of women competing for his attention and no drama. Was I on the cusp of finally making the right call when it came to men?

A few weeks into 2006, I decided to have 'the talk'. I needed to be upfront with LNT on a few personal matters before things went too far and either of us got hurt unnecessarily.

'Honey,' I began, 'I need to discuss three things if we're going to make this long term.'

He nodded, prepared for whatever I had to say.

'Firstly, I have a neurological disease that shows itself under stress, and I'm not sure how it will play out in the future.'

Silence filled the space between us as he processed my words, and I could see him reflecting on what I'd said. After what felt like an eternity, he broke the silence with a response that was more than I could have hoped for.

'That just makes me love you more. You're all the more remarkable.'

'Secondly, I can't promise I won't want more children.'

He drifted into quiet reflection again and then smiled. 'That's good to know as I feel the same way.'

I took a deep breath, then dropped the bomb.

'This is the clincher,' I said in a barely audible voice. 'I have something that is difficult to share, and I hope you can forgive me...'

I could see the colour drain from his face as his eyes filled with the kind of dread that comes just before a calamitous event unfolds. Then, with perfect timing, I let fly with a Guinness World Record-worthy fart, one so exceptional that it left us both gasping for air in the thick hazy trail of toxic fumes that promised to linger around the room for hours.

'I am so glad I got that out the way,' I chortled. 'I needed to know I can fully relax with you.'

'What a relief,' a clearly reassured LNT spluttered, probably with his eyes stinging in the aftermath. He gave me a half-smile, clearly trying to hold back a laugh – or maybe he was just trying to hold his breath! It was as if in that cathartic moment, I'd crossed some kind of invisible boundary. He was finally seeing the real me, the me who had allowed the walls to come down and wasn't afraid to be imperfect.

The next thing I knew, LNT was moving in and true to form, there was nothing flash or ostentatious about his arrival.

A few weeks later, we got our first official couple invite to the wedding of one of my former Club 18-30 colleagues. She was marrying a holidaying punter who she'd fallen in love with during those wild Turkish days. The wedding was at the luxurious Cameron House Hotel on the serene banks of Scotland's Loch Lomond, just a stone's throw from where we decided to stay at a very posh mansion owned by a friend's parents. The mansion's absolute grandeur was only enhanced by the fact that it had once been the home of *Wet Wet Wet* lead singer, Marti Pellow.

LNT and I arrived a few days early and used the time to explore the beautiful surrounding hills. One chilly morning as we wandered along, I spotted a lamb perched precariously on the side of a steep cliff. It stared back at me with what I interpreted to be an I've-been-here-for-most-of-my-young-life-and-am-starving-to-death look. My maternal instincts kicked in.

'We have to rescue him, we just have to,' I wailed to LNT. 'You must save this poor baby...'

Ever the chivalrous man, he said nothing but set off toward the 'lambsel' in distress, cautiously navigating the perilous descent down the hill face. From my vantage point, I could see that approaching the lamb from below and climbing up was the smarter, safer route. I called out to LNT to share my discovery of an easier path and he nodded in agreement, changing his plan to close in on the lamb. But before he could reach it, the ungrateful little creature shot him a look that could only be described as 'pillock' before bouncing down the cliff with the calm assurance of someone who'd been doing this their whole life. LNT meanwhile was left dangling, his feet scrambling for solid ground. The reality now struck me, the cheeky little fucker wasn't a lamb at all but a confident, assertive mountain goat. The nerve of it! If I'd been armed, I swear I would've blown its smug head off right then and there, sending it express delivery to the Pearly Gates.

My murderous thoughts were interrupted when it dawned on me that LNT was stuck in a classic Catch-22 situation. Going up was very dangerous and going down was insane without a safety harness. There was no option left but to call for help. I dialled 999 in a frenzy and within minutes a super-efficient rescue team arrived. They quickly assessed the situation and set into motion a slick plan to rescue the spanner – aka LNT. His self-esteem took one final battering when I told the rescuers it was all his silly idea because he didn't know the difference between a lamb and a goat.

The wedding reception later that evening had all my Club 18-30 peers together on a large round table as far removed from the civilised guests as possible. The air was thick with conversation, mostly of the 'war story' variety. One former Club Rep took delight in reminding me and the others of my, *ahem*, less than pristine reputation.

'Oh my God,' she yelled looking over at me. 'Do we remember Barbie?'

I rolled my eyes half-laughing, half-wincing at the reminder of my past, but I did appreciate the fact that in that moment, I was surrounded by people who knew me well, even if some of them were holding on to the more colourful parts of my history. I turned my eyes to LNT where I observed him shifting nervously in his seat. He knew a bit about my past but clearly sensed there was more to the executive summary than had been previously divulged.

The ex-Club Rep yeller was not about to disappoint. 'We were at the hen's night in Manchester last week, watching videos of Turkey,' she began. 'And there you were, emceeing the endurance test on the beach that day. Remember the game where the guys had to stand barefoot on beer crates, covered in baby oil, in their swim shorts, all while enduring fifty-degree Celsius temperatures?' She grinned at me, clearly relishing the moment. 'You remember what you told them you'd do if they won?' she asked, her tone implying there was no chance I could forget.

I gave the gentlest of nods, my face already flushed with embarrassment.

'You remember that?' LNT asked, this time with no pretense of subtlety. His voice laced with genuine curiosity, as I felt a twinge of anxiety.

Once again, I meekly nodded. Meanwhile, the yeller delighted the table with stories about how these men had volunteered for the original *Celebrity Get Me Out of Here* – the beach edition – where they were blindfolded and fed different levels of pain food, from chili to cat food. The stories kept coming, always with my lewd antics taking centre stage and each bringing me more anxiety.

It dawned on me that LNT's first real encounter with my wild past was on the same day when, just that morning, he'd offered me a rehearsal proposal – minus the ring – very sweetly and gently.

'I know you fear marriage and I understand that you don't want to get married right now,' he had said softly as we did the tourist thing and strolled along the banks of Loch Ness, gazing out at the mist slowly drifting skywards. 'But if you tell me you will marry me one day, that's all I need.'

It was a moment of breathtaking beauty – the words in perfect harmony with the serene surroundings. I knew then, without a doubt, that this was real. He was my happily ever after. There was no pressure, no rush, and in that moment, I was one hundred per cent sure. I stopped in my tracks, turned to face him and with all the certainty I had, said, 'Absolutely, yes.'

Now, just a few hours after becoming his unofficial fiancée, I found myself in the spotlight for all the wrong reasons again. I cursed myself for ever thinking it was a good idea to bring LNT to an ex-Club 18-30 Rep wedding.

'Shitfuckbollockwank, I think I have blown it – I can't see our relationship surviving this,' I muttered to myself.

In an effort to drown the awkwardness, I hit the champagne hard and by the time we returned to our palatial room, I was horribly drunk. I proceeded to deposit a regrettable portion of my Beef Wellington dinner into the basin before falling into bed. Through my drunken haze, I could see LNT dutifully pushing the chunks down the plughole before rinsing and cleaning the basin so he could brush his teeth.

'He's a fucking keeper, he is,' I said to myself while clutching a thumping head.

LNT's patience was once again tested during a romantic holiday in the humid heat of the Dominican Republic a few months later. We landed on a particularly sweltering day and climbed aboard a bus only to learn from the driver that we had a three-hour journey ahead of us. The winding, bumpy tracks in a vehicle that pre-dated Noah's Ark were sure to push my car-sickness affliction to its limits.

I did what I could to counter it by choosing a seat near the front of the bus, hoping for the best. However, my resolve was quickly tested when I noticed a teenage girl on the opposite aisle. She looked pasty and sweaty, holding a cloth over her mouth as her entire body convulsed. The sight triggered the first spurt of bile in my mouth and I silently cursed my fragile stomach.

'I'm going to be sick,' I told LNT, my voice shaky as I clutched the seat in front of me. He immediately sprang into action, rubbing my back soothingly in an attempt to distract me from a road clearly laid by people who have since been executed for their incompetence.

It was too late – the stomach contractions now consumed my every move and my eyes glowed red as if possessed by the devil. LNT, ever the calm one, managed to secure a plastic bag from the young girl's mum and pass it to me just as I re-enacted the basin scene from the *Wet Wet Wet* mansion. This time I added my best high-energy *Iron Maiden* performance to the scene as my loud, violent and mammoth spew deposited litres of sickly bile into the bag. The feel of warm liquid crawling over my feet had me look down to see the bag full of safety holes, apparently to prevent suffocation.

'For fuck's sake, we now have a puke sprinkler system,' I slurred to LNT, my mouth and nose dripping with puke.

As the bus bounced over the rutted road, each jolt sent the spewed vomit spiralling down the aisle toward the rear of the bus leaving a trail of suffering in its wake. The stench became unbearable, and my puke seemed to trigger a chain reaction among my fellow passengers. A Mexican Wave of vomit-volleys spread through the bus, quickly transforming the aisle into Barf Boulevard.

Amidst a bus awash with carrot chunks and misery at just twenty minutes into its lengthy journey, one person stood as a beacon of composure – LNT. The cool composure he maintained, despite the horrendous situation, left no room for doubt.

'He's a fucking keeper,' I whispered to myself, clutching my sick bag full of lumps and trying to keep it from dripping the newly strained liquid onto my feet.

> *Mr Right needed to not just accept my past but embrace it as an integral part of who I was. LNT saw the clown and chose to stay in the circus – offering acceptance rather than judgment. Love isn't about perfection; it's about understanding and appreciating the journey that has shaped who we are.*

15

Blow Job

Have you ever bumped into someone you haven't seen for a while and notice a new-found happiness in them before they even speak a word?

I recall seeing her leaving the family court alone with fists clenched in triumph. There was a raw elation on her face as she marched forward, her head tilted back and mouth wide open as if ready to catch rain drops. In that moment she screamed, 'Yeeessssssss!' Her unrestrained joy was palpable, and it was clear that she felt liberated from the weight of a long and painful chapter. 'She' was Nicole Kidman, who it seemed wasn't aware that the cameras were there to capture the moment and share it with the world. Her divorce from her own Lord Farquaard was now finalised and what had once been a deeply personal battle had now become public fodder.

Back then, watching that moment unfold on the TV, I felt like shouting at the screen, 'Get a grip, girl!' How bad could it have been being married to Tom Cruise? Granted he's a bit short, but he's an extremely rich and good-looking Lord Farquaad.

It wasn't until my fateful day in 2006 that I truly understood Nicole Kidman's reaction. I was at home when I received the call informing me that my *Decree Absolute* would liberate me the next day. In that instant, everything changed. I dropped to my knees as my grasp on the phone loosened and it fell with a soft thud onto the carpet. My fists clenched, my head went back, and I howled into the air. I wailed uncontrollably, tears streaming down my face as the weight I didn't even know I had been carrying was finally released. I had never wailed like that before; such was the relief. The news of the imminent arrival of the divorce papers was setting me free. It was an intoxicating cocktail of happiness, signalling the removal of those invisible shackles at last.

The very next day, I found myself contemplating the start of the next phase of my life. I had made a conscious decision to navigate the divorce process on my own to avoid carrying the drama of the past into my future. Now I felt I could properly start my new life with LNT...

James, now an adult, largely independent, and a terrific son, had successfully finished school and enrolled in a Sport Science program at college. With that phase of motherhood behind me, my thoughts turned to the idea of having baby number two – this time with LNT.

Pregnancy happened the first time we decided not to use protection. At thirty-six years old I felt incredibly blessed.

On the professional front, a series of well-celebrated promotions led me to a coveted understudy position with one of my all-time favourite bosses, Rick. He was one of the two gentlemen who had interviewed me the day I wore my don't-fuck-with-me Bonnie and Clyde outfit. Impressed by my performance, he had told me that he would create a new role for me – and he kept his word. Now in a high-powered position overseeing a large region in the UK, Rick was an inspiration. A small, slightly eccentric man in his fifties, he hired me to write a series of People Plans for the various divisions under his leadership. Once I had completed this daunting task to his satisfaction, Rick showered me with praise and complimented me on my deep understanding of rewards and sanctions within the prison environment.

'You have nailed it,' Rick told me at my annual review. 'This is the very essence of a forward-thinking scheme that will transform our approach and go a long way towards enhancing prisoner behaviour. In fact, it's so good, I would like to second you to the European Union Twinning

Commission. How would you feel about joining them in Romania next month to investigate local operations and collectively write the country's first ever prisoner behavioural reward scheme?'

A swell of pride rose within me as Rick shared his praise. I nodded eagerly determined not to disappoint and immediately threw myself into researching the Romanian penal system. It was starkly different from the one I worked in. It was how I imagined the UK system might have looked in the sixties – many male prisoners with shaven heads, little interaction observed between staff and inmates, and overcrowded conditions. The prison officers in Romania were similar to their British counterparts, but I noticed greater responsibility for interacting with prisoners falling on psychologists rather than on the prison officers. While I could see the value of having trained psychologists communicating with inmates, I was left wondering if the officers did more than just unlock and lock doors. I felt an overwhelming sense of pride that those in our prisons in the UK seemed in many ways far better off than their counterparts in the Balkans.

When the day came to leave for Romania, my recently accumulated knowledge of Romanian society almost went to waste as my life flashed before me when our pilot made a hairy approach into the country. It was minus eighteen degrees Celsius on the ground. My nose was pressed to the aircraft window as I took in the eerily beautiful frozen landscape below, bathed in a blanket of snow as a brooding opaque sky watched over it. I heard the wheels release from the undercarriage and eased back in my seat to prepare for landing. Just then, the plane collided with what I was later told was a pocket of frozen fog. The aircraft lurched wildly, passenger screams filled the cabin and looks of absolute terror were evident on the faces of the flight attendants. The plane shuddered and convulsed as the pilot aborted the landing, desperately attempting to pull the aircraft into an ascent. Pandemonium followed as the oxygen masks dropped from the overhead compartments and the sounds of screaming and wailing intensified around me as we sat frozen by fear. My heart raced and I was convinced that this was it – the end. There was no way this pressurised tin can could safely land on its wheels, taxi to the exit gates and bid everyone a cheery, 'Welcome, thank you for flying Bob-the-Builder Airways.'

In those moments of pure panic, I can vouch that you truly take stock of your life and what it all means. Tears streamed down my face as I reached over to the stranger in the seat next to me. A man in his early sixties with hands like shovels, he had a depraved look that suggested he enjoyed pulling the wings off flies. However, I was determined not to die without holding someone's hand and I grabbed his with a vice-like grip. Just then, the aircraft shook, heaved upward and started to gain altitude. Shortly afterwards, a crackle of the intercom system then a voice told us all was well. The skilled captain had successfully completed this heroic manoeuvre and went on to land safely to rapturous applause from all the passengers.

Romania was an eye-opener. My first familiarisation tour of the city's prison revealed a world where each six-foot by four-foot cell had just two beds on top of one another. Describing the two beds as a bunkbed was a slight exaggeration, as there was only about half of the usual space between the top and bottom bed. Each cell I visited housed more than two inmates and although I wasn't too fancy at maths, I knew two beds wasn't going to cut it when the lights went out. I asked the prisoners in one cell how they slept and was surprised to learn that they took it in turns. Those awake only had room to stand bolt upright in their cramped cell and dream of the horizontal hours while awaiting their turn.

The cell occupants were visibly startled to see a woman inspecting their quarters. And not just any woman, but a heavily pregnant English woman. The fact that she appeared to have a bit of clout was another unusual element for these felons to digest. I looked long and hard at each of them and saw they were largely expressionless as if all emotion had been sucked from their eyes. The hollowness that stared back at me was unsettling – a silent reflection of the lives these imprisoned men had endured. It spoke volumes about the emotional weight of their existence behind bars. Yet, despite this overwhelming emptiness, there was one small outlet they could cling to – a mobile phone. It wasn't much, but it offered a fleeting connection to the outside world, allowing them to reach out to loved ones and remind them that even though they were locked away and out of sight, they were still alive.

The mobile phone is ordinarily a symbol of wholesome connection, but in prison, it had become a tool for blurring the lines between law and order. In prisons around the globe, the mobile phone was contraband, and the discovery of one carried significant consequences. These forbidden tools had become powerful weapons, enabling prisoners to continue their criminal activities from behind bars. It's widely known that, despite the stoic effort of staff, mobile phones get smuggled into prison and are often used to orchestrate drug deliveries. These transactions are often carefully hidden using creative methods like drugs being concealed in baby's nappies, which as a parent, still blows my mind.

I was intrigued by the senior Romanian official's insistence that mobile phones weren't an issue in their prisons, especially considering how widespread the problem had become worldwide.

'We don't have a mobile phone problem here,' he had assured me confidently.

'Oh, come on,' I replied. 'It's pretty much a global issue these days. Why should your prisoners be any different from others around the world?'

He reiterated, 'Ma'am, let me repeat: We do not have a mobile phone problem in our prisons here.'

Just a couple of days later as I sat sipping a less than rewarding hotel coffee, my gaze landed on a national newspaper. My gasp was audible when I saw the front page, which featured a shocking photo emblazoned across it. A shaven headed prisoner had his tongue hanging out, with his cell mate's knob snugly in his mouth. It was all captured on a mobile phone camera by, I assumed, a third prisoner, and shared with the digital community beyond the prison walls. I didn't need to be fluent in any language to understand what those men were saying. They were bored shitless and left with no choice but to create their own entertainment.

'Prison sucks!' they screamed with the help of the local tabloid headline.

Needing a hit of caffeine, I bravely downed the rank coffee, pulled on my fleece-lined jacket and made my way to work. As luck would have it, the first person I saw was the senior official who had been adamant about being the only country in the world where mobile phones aren't smuggled into prisons. He was sitting outside with the daily paper resting on his knees, and as I approached, he looked up. Our eyes met and we held each other's gaze for a moment. I felt a little unsettled given our recent discussions and I hoped he didn't think I had orchestrated the headline to prove a point. But to his credit, he remained open to a suggestion of mine that aimed to improve the lives of prisoners. I proposed calling a meeting of the prison's senior executives to discuss the creation of a Prisoner Incentives and Privileges policy. I emphasised that it was crucial for prisoner representatives to be involved in the discussion. The reaction was intense. Silence filled the room. The void of voices was palpable. I could feel the weight of this change in practice, but I gently explained my reasoning for stronger collaboration in decisions that affect the lives of prisoners.

My no-problem-with-mobile-phones guy was first to endorse my approach, paving the way for everyone to nod and agree. From that time forth, prisoner representatives attended the policy development meetings. When the first two prisoners arrived at the inaugural meeting, they looked like petrified rabbits caught in the headlights. Clearly, they were out of their depth and uncomfortable in the presence of senior staff. This was a completely foreign experience for them. However, as the discussion progressed, they began to warm to the task. Their contributions turned out to be invaluable. It was one of the most fulfilling moments of my career, knowing that together we had made a tangible, positive impact on the lives of over 12,000 humans, as well as on the many people working within the Romanian prison system.

Professionally content and filled with anticipation, I headed home.

My heart was brimming with excitement as I prepared for the arrival of our baby. I envisioned a home filled with warmth and laughter – a sanctuary where our newborn would grow surrounded by love, stability and the presence of both a mum and a dad. It was a traditional vision perhaps, but one that was meaningful to me, especially with the added blessing of a now nineteen-year-old James still living with us. It was a vision grounded in the simplicity of a home filled with love.

Patience had never been one of my strong suits. I rushed through life eager for the next big thing, never fully allowing myself to appreciate the present moment. Much had changed, and I stood on a new stage. I had learnt the lesson the hard way because I hadn't been prepared to listen. Now I realised that the most meaningful changes came when I let life unfold on its own timeline.

16

Volcano Vagina

I swear there are moments when I'm the lead role in some absurd sitcom about a traveling circus, and the circus is my life. From being holed up in an infectious diseases ward one minute, to climbing a volcano the next, I wondered if it was even safe to leave the house. It's like the universe had a fluorescent sign flashing in my face that read, 'Hey knobhead, yes you... we're talking about you.'

On falling pregnant, I was super excited and couldn't wait to share the news with my son James – though he threw me a little when he screwed up his face in a manner reserved exclusively for teenagers. His spontaneous reply was, 'Ewwww Mum, that's gross!'

In his defence, most teenagers do battle to come to terms with the reality that their mothers have a sex life. Once he'd got over the fact that I must have had sex at least once in the previous four months, his facial expression morphed into one of love. He was a great support throughout my pregnancy and gifted me one of the most cherished compliments of my life.

'Mum, I am nineteen, I have been an only child all those years and you have spoilt me rotten. So why shouldn't you do it all again? After all, you're a great mother.'

Telling my parents was a different matter altogether. Despite being thirty-six, I still felt apprehensive about sharing the news with them. I feared it might dredge up a flood of painful memories, reducing me to a child once again. I couldn't help but worry about how they would judge me this time. The anxiety deepened as I reflected on the unresolved hurt from when I was sixteen. Their disapproval back then had marked the beginning of their long line of unfavourable judgments on the decisions I made throughout my life. Given that, I had every reason to believe that the news of a second child – again out of wedlock, though under very different circumstances – would be met with negativity.

Unable to bear the thought of enduring another round of being called a 'silly, silly girl', my dread led me to take what might be considered a gutless approach. I decided to share my joyful news in a letter to Mum and Dad. I didn't want those whose love I longed for the most to say something that would haunt me for the rest of my life – especially when I was certain that having another child was the next step in what had become my now perfect life.

I stared at the blank piece of paper for what felt like hours, chewing on the back of my pen as I carefully crafted the letter in my head. Once I was sure I had it right, I felt ready to begin writing...

Dear Mum and Dad, I would like to start by telling you that I love you both very much and I know you feel I have let you down before. For the first time I feel like I am in control of my life. I am truly happy. Your endorsement of my decisions now – as my parents – means everything. I have chosen to write to you, to enable you to digest what I am about to say, especially as I do not want you to respond with anything negative that none of us can either undo or forget.

LNT and I are having a baby. We are delighted. The baby was planned and will be very much loved. Please give me a call when you are ready. I love you both very much. Your daughter.

I longed for their blessing, desperately needing them to tell me they were delighted with the news. But the response didn't come immediately and the week that followed felt like an eternity. Then, the landline phone rang. Since no one else ever called the landline, I knew instantly it was Mum. I answered the call with a nervous, 'Hello?'

'Hello, we got your letter,' Mum said, her voice carrying an untranslatable tone.

I didn't speak, waiting for her to continue. She in turn, remained silent, likely waiting for me to respond. The silence hung heavily before she finally said, 'Congratulations.'

I sensed it was not easy for her to say and appreciated the effort she had made. 'Thank you, Mum, it means a lot to me,' I replied.

We both breathed a sigh of relief. The taboo subject of pregnancy out of wedlock had been broached, albeit at a *really* high-level. We could now shift the discussion to uncomplicated topics like the weather – that obligatory digression so common in British conversations. My relief was palpable.

At twelve weeks into the pregnancy, I woke up in the middle of the night feeling something wet beneath me. 'Oh shit, I've wet the bloody bed,' my sleepy brain suggested.

Then, with growing alarm, another thought hit me. 'Oh fuck, maybe my waters have broken.'

As unpleasant as the idea of pee-drenched bedding was, it paled into insignificance compared with the enormity of my waters breaking at twelve weeks. The relief that washed over me when I realised I wasn't dealing with amniotic fluid but rather a pool of my own shit was almost comical.

I jumped up in a manner reminiscent of Spud from the movie *Trainspotting,* flinging shit in all directions. LNT wasn't spared as I hopped, kangaroo-style towards the bathroom. Unlike the Greek shit encounter of my younger days that was executed with military precision, this one completely caught me off guard. There was no time to grab toilet paper – this was a spontaneous sleep-shit combustion, seeping out of my bum like a thief in the night. I silently scolded my incompetent sphincter for its failure to perform its primary duty.

As I dealt with the aftermath, I noticed LNT stirring, rubbing his shit-spattered eyes and asking, 'What's that smell?'

'Sorry, Honey,' I whispered while surveying my handywork. 'Erm, I've shat the bed, and you've got some on your face.'

Ever my rock, LNT sat up, switched on the bedside lamp and took in the scene before slowly lifting his weary body from the bed. He ambled over to the wardrobe mirror, took one look and said, 'So I have,' in his usual calm manner. He grabbed a tissue and methodically wiped his Dalmatian-like shit-spotted face while reassuring me, 'Everything's fine. You're clearly not well – clean yourself up and I'll call the doctor.'

It sounded like a perfectly sensible next step and as I entered the shower cubicle, I caught a glimpse of the wonderful man in my life stripping the bed, rolling up the linen and placing it in the corner. As always, he didn't flinch as he slipped into autopilot and set about making things right.

'He *is* a fucking keeper,' I told myself, as I turned on the shower tap and sent shit scurrying down the drainpipe.

As the jets of water cleansed me, my mind drifted. I wondered if perhaps LNT had some underlying mental health issues that drew him to me. Just then, as if he could read my thoughts, he glanced over in my direction.

'I love you, Honey, even if you have now literally shat all over me,' he chuckled.

It was very comforting to know that there wasn't much I could do to shock him or deter him from wanting to spend the rest of his life with me.

Soon after I got out of the shower, the doctor arrived. He poked and prodded and asked a series of questions. He eventually concluded I needed antibiotics. When I told him I was allergic to penicillin, he found he didn't have the right medicine with him and instructed me to go to hospital for treatment. Without hesitating, we quickly got ready and headed to the nearest hospital.

Upon arrival, I was greeted by an awaiting medical team who swiftly whisked me away for numerous tests, none of which could diagnose the unwelcome bug thought to be nesting in my body.

After a hefty wait, a visiting specialist absolutely floored me when he declared in a matter-of-fact tone, 'Your early-stage pregnancy and allergy to penicillin limit our ability to treat you. You'll need to stay with us for a while and you will be confined to an infectious diseases ward while we grow your faeces in the hospital's laboratory.'

The isolation in the infectious diseases ward induced waves of boredom, and I paced around dreaming up activities to relieve the tedium. Never one for card games, it was a relief when I was eventually deemed safe to roam the hospital corridors. I took great delight in peeking into rooms and chatting with various patients.

My spirits were further lifted when I stumbled across a prisoner in the ward opposite me. Ever the dutiful public servant and with little else to do while waiting for my poo to grow mushrooms, I figured I could help Her Majesty's cause by checking in on this tuberculosis-inflicted chap every day. It was a mutually beneficial arrangement – I could quell my boredom at the same time as ensuring he was properly cuffed – as is the requirement of being a governor.

My meanderings ended when the correct antibiotic was found and intravenously administered over the next four days. I soon recovered from the nasty and hitherto indestructible *E-coli* bug and, aside from growing to the size of a boutique hotel – with my feet and ankles transformed into chankles – it was a hassle-free pregnancy with a hairy surprise at its conclusion.

Our daughter Amy was two-and-a-half weeks overdue and I had to be induced. If you have ever had a baby induced, you'll relate to the sensation of a human's arm pushed up your vagina while their hand clutches a long crochet hook to break your waters. When contractions don't follow, they wire you up to a drug that quickly takes things from zero to hero. At T-minus sixty seconds, there's barely time for a few puffs of gas before the pain hits – its fucking horrific.

I knew from experience that overindulging in gas could quickly alter the mind in a way not unlike smoking cannabis; consequently, I sucked in as much as I could. The effect was immediate, and I suddenly took on the persona of a transvestite named Crystal. A freaked-out LNT looked on as one of the student doctors – a clone of Mark from Take That – attempted to deal with my delusions. I couldn't help myself. Every time I saw him, I broke into song. *All I do each night is pray, hoping that you'll be a part of me again someday.*

'Surely I can't still be high?' I asked LNT when I first laid eyes on Amy.

What I saw was a face only a mother could love – a face that looked like it belonged to the Neanderthal age, completely covered in black hair.

'Oh, my God!' I gasped as her tiny mouth emitted sounds more fitting for a hungry guinea pig. 'Her father is beautiful, and I certainly don't look like something from *Planet of the Apes*,' I added, glancing over at the midwife, hoping there had been some sort of mix-up and this was someone else's child.

I tried to be positive, searching for beauty beneath the fur coating but I just couldn't find it. In a moment of light-hearted escapism, I wondered if maybe some alien had accosted me during one of my sleepwalking episodes and fathered this bushy little creature. I even briefly entertained the idea of distracting the nursery staff long enough to pull off a baby swap! Amy was not a looker, not even through the eyes of a doting mother. But LNT? From the moment he laid eyes on her, he was completely smitten with the fluffy kitten. To him, his hairy daughter was the most beautiful thing he had ever set eyes on.

I cautiously made my way to the shower to inspect the collateral damage to my tired and battered nether region. I was nervous to touch it as

I knew birthing a nine-pound baby would have cosmetically catastrophic implications. Filled with apprehension, I grabbed the shower head and positioned it hovering upside down facing my broken vagina like a metal detector. As the jets of water hit the newly formed Grand Canyon, I wondered whether I could join a choir as a backstage pan-pipe lead. There was no doubt that I would have to get my pelvic floor muscles working again if I ever wanted to travel on a motorbike, ride a rollercoaster or even sit on the beach on a windy day... unless I fancied being the first human air balloon.

That night as the little monkey was placed in her cot, I tried to do a runner but was caught and dragged back to fulfil my maternal duties. I'm kidding... sort of. We both managed to get some much-needed sleep and when I woke up clean and refreshed the next morning, she looked a lot cuter... especially when I plonked a pink balaclava on her head and pulled it over her face. As the days passed, the ape-like fur rubbed off revealing a big-eyed, cute-as-a-button angel.

Seven months of maternity leave followed, providing some of the most enjoyable moments of my life.

With Pompeii high on my bucket list, our first family trip was to Italy when Amy was just four weeks old. Each day the brooding Mount Vesuvius towered over us and one morning, LNT looked up at this volcanic mass and suggested we should climb it.

'Fucking hell,' I gasped as we reached the summit. 'What is so special about climbing a frigging volcano?'

The answer came swiftly as LNT bent down on one knee, reached his right hand into his jacket pocket and nervously pulled out a small, padded box. He opened it to reveal a sparkling diamond solitaire engagement ring.

'Will you marry me?' he asked.

After chastising him for making me climb a volcano that had me doing a little wee with every step, I didn't hesitate. 'Hell yes,' I replied.

We were living the dream as a new family, and I truly believed I had finally found happiness.

As humans, we use history – both personal and shared – to guide us in predicting the future. Yet it's never an exact science. People can be unpredictable, their actions and emotions sometimes surprising even to themselves. It's this unpredictability that makes life so interesting. Being curious is what makes us grow as humans. We need to ask ourselves, 'What else might be true?'

17

The Lady in Red

I wasn't even safe from ridiculousness on my commute to work – one minute I've got a dream job, the next I'm strutting the streets of London covered in soot and acne having just spent the last hour in a pool of piss and misguided optimism.

Post Amy's birth and a month into my maternity leave, my tummy had become more of a blancmange than a 'gunt' and my chankles regained their rightful ankle and calf proportions. Feeling almost ready to take on the world again, I opted to spend three days in the office as part of the organisation's 'Keeping in Touch' program.

Those twenty-four work hours turned out to deliver the most exciting career change I had ever dreamed of.

While shuffling around the office reacquainting myself with its workings, my boss Rick announced his billy-big-potatoes promotion. It was a newly created post to oversee the merger of two organisations – Prisons and Probation. I congratulated him on his promotion and jokingly said he would have to spruce up his corporate wardrobe if he was to fit into the London set with its reputation for style.

Rick was a guardian angel in my professional world, occupying the same treasured space as Hank before him. I was genuinely happy for him but saddened by the thought of losing him from my working life.

'Thank you,' Rick replied. 'I am sure my fashion sense will be just fine as I would like you to join me.'

'What?' I exclaimed, dumbfounded at the magnitude of the proposition put to me. I struggled to restrain my inner wildcat from jumping onto his head and screaming with sheer delight.

'Do you want to be my Chief of Staff?' super-boss Rick asked.

'Errrr, yeeahhh,' I blurted, without a hint of hesitation.

I hadn't fully considered the implications. I hadn't thought about what it would mean to trade a casual thirty-minute car ride to work in Oxford for a two-hour each way, multi-train commute into London. In a rush, I returned home to share the news with a delighted LNT, who was wise enough to know that this was a massive career opportunity for me – the job of a lifetime in our profession.

'We will make this work,' he assured me, pulling me in for a bear hug.

We were always good at making things work. Each morning, I caught the six o'clock train into London while LNT dropped Amy off at the local nursery on the way to his workplace and picked her up again at just before seven o'clock in the evening. It was exhausting but our unwavering support for each other, paired with a sense of blissful happiness saw us through.

As Rick's Staff Officer – prison parlance for Chief of Staff – I was responsible for managing most aspects of his professional life. He oversaw around thirty thousand offenders across London, supported by roughly nine thousand staff. It was a mega-gig, which meant my day started at four o'clock with the in-your-face ring of my bedside alarm clock. I'd start by attending to Amy, then walk for thirty minutes to catch the stupid o'clock train out of Oxford heading to Paddington. From there I'd switch trains to Oxford Circus where another transfer put me on the train to Pimlico. Once there, I'd briskly walk for another twenty minutes to the offices in Westminster, and at the end of the day, reverse the process. It was a hectic routine, but the saying, *Choose a job you love and you will never work a day in your life*, is so very true. I loved every second of my job.

In the early days, I would hop on the train in high spirits, sporting a big, cheery smile and ready to greet my fellow commuters with a nod and a wave. Almost all of them responded with cold, bewildered stares, clearly puzzled by what they considered odd behaviour. I reasoned that their reaction was a result of years spent enduring the lonely, uninviting commute. It seemed that on British public transport, the unwritten rule was to bury your face in a newspaper or a book and totally ignore those around you. Those without something to read would either stare out of the window into the blackness or down at the floor – basically, anywhere but at the face of a fellow human being. Miserable buggers, I thought. But I was determined to keep my smile and maintain my cheery disposition.

My mission hit a bump one morning, halfway between home and London, when I spotted a seriously inebriated man sitting on the floor by the carriage entrance. I locked eyes with him and smiled, only for him to respond by unleashing a barrage of profanities.

'Shhhtuppid, fuuuucking, shhtupppid, you shhhit shhhturing shhhlut,' he slurred.

I nodded to acknowledge that I had at least deciphered some of his barrage, in the hope that he would turn his attention towards someone else. Instead, he slowly lifted himself from the floor, grabbed at and missed the handrail and crashed in a heap on the seat next to me. Too drunk to bear any malice, he looked up at me with a creased face that told of a life of hard knocks. He offered a faint, toothless smile before falling asleep, leaving me staring at his thick Barbour waterproof mac, half-open and now brushing against my bare left leg.

Suddenly, the mac triggered a memory of a trip to Amsterdam a few years earlier. On that occasion, a flight attendant friend and I had inadvertently linked up with a group of twenty-one British men on a stag weekend. A little unorthodox perhaps, but she hooked up with the groom. One of our outings took us to a sex show at a seedy venue in the city's red-light district. The smoky room was full of mostly middle-aged white men in dusty trench-coats, much like the one worn by my drunken train companion. During the show, the star attraction delivered a fittingly stellar performance, executing an intricate scissor routine midway through and while her legs were splayed apart, she popped a cigar into her vagina. She lit it and proceeded to inhale and exhale, blowing smoke rings into the audience.

'Bloody marvellous,' my 'when in Amsterdam' stoned brain yelled, and I was up on my feet clapping loudly while the trench coat brigade looked on. They had probably seen the show before... many times.

It's perhaps unsurprising that we missed our flight home, thanks to some hash cupcakes, but we managed to catch the next one a couple of hours later. My flight attendant friend got chatty with one of the other guys from the stag party after Stag Man had wisely come to his senses. She actually ended up marrying the second guy not long after. I made sure to bring popcorn to her wedding in case any secrets came out of the vault, as Stag Man – whom she'd slept with in Amsterdam – was the Best Man, attending with his unsuspecting new wife.

My fond flashback was interrupted as the train jolted around a bend and the pissed purveyor of profanities lolled about like a ragdoll, his gritty mop of hair coming to rest in my lap. As I gently lifted him back upright, I heard what I thought was a downpour of rain. A quick glance out at the clear blue skies made it perfectly clear – no, it wasn't rain – it was the sound of this guy wetting himself in his sleep, and it running down his mac – dangerously close to my leg – then onto the floor.

A growing puddle beneath his seat confirmed my suspicions. I lifted my bag and feet off the floor so as not to be tainted by his eighty per cent proof piss. As I did, my fellow commuters briefly acknowledged my existence with fleeting eye contact. But it wasn't out of solidarity or support. One man's piercing glare unmistakably said, 'That's wiped the stupid smile off your face, hasn't it!'

Sadly, the episode served to reinforce the London transport mantra that you never look anyone in the eye. And there, in that moment, involuntarily and reluctantly, I had to become one of them – a London train zombie...

The train journey became a kind of research session, offering great insight into the sociological behaviour of the bored commuter. My people-watching was well rewarded when an attractive young woman jumped aboard one rainy September morning. Immaculately dressed in a beautifully tailored black suit, offset by a stylish pair of red shoes, she turned heads as she made her way to a vacant row of seats a few paces ahead of me.

A mischievous looking guy got on at the next stop and as fate would have it, he took the empty seat next to her and struck up a conversation. I reckon he had heard the *Lady in Red* song – not the Chris de Burgh genteel version but the more raucous Club 18-30 version we'd chant on the four-hour bus ride from the airport to the resort. It went something along the lines of, *There's a lady in red, who likes to give good head...*

The small talk must have worked, as they sat together each day after that. By the fourth day, they snuck off to the bathroom together, only to return a couple of minutes later slightly dishevelled and rosy-cheeked. 'Come on mate, surely you can do better than that,' I muttered under my breath as he made his way back to his seat.

The next day he upped his game, stretching it to about five minutes. By the following week, he crashed through the eight-minute barrier, then hit a personal best just a few days later. Each day, as our Lady in Red and her Christian Grey headed for their rendezvous, I'd amuse myself by humming the old Club 18-30 ditty, silently chuckling at the crude lyrics that followed. *The Lady in Black who takes it on her back. The Lady in White who never stays the night. The Lady in Green likes it rough and mean. The Lady in Glitter who takes it up the...* Let's just say, I hope that one coincided with his birthday!

My voyeuristic venture came to an end at the start of the third week when Christian Grey failed to board the train. I was tempted to ask her what had happened, but I had noticed they both wore wedding rings, so I thought better of it. I suspect he was on a training course in London for a few weeks and opportunity knocked. Their liaison did serve as a reminder of just how lucky I was. I was in a happy relationship with a wonderful man, and we had a baby daughter who had rapidly evolved from ape to girl in just a few weeks.

My inspiring boss ensured my workdays were filled with stimulating challenges, especially in my role overseeing anti-corruption and counterterrorism efforts. My team focused on identifying prisoners who had either been radicalised or were vulnerable to it. The intelligence we gleaned enabled us to do everything we could to ensure that when these individuals were finally released into the community, our justice partners had a complete picture of who they were.

Like my boss Rick, I was also seduced by London's fashion and had splashed out on a tailored white linen suit. The next morning, I strutted around the bedroom in my new attire, admiring its finery and ability to bring out the best in me. Standing on the train platform in my finest linen, I felt the familiar swoosh of back-drafted air blow through my hair as the train approached, its breeze adding a Marilyn Monroe moment to my idyllic world.

I boarded the crowded train, hoping to catch the eye of a seated gentleman who might offer his seat to a trendy young professional woman. But no one fitted the description of a gentleman, and no one budged. As I clung to the germ-infested vertical handrail, I surreptitiously scanned my fellow passengers only to receive the customary blank stares from those daring enough to make eye contact. However, when I made it to work, I was greeted by several long and deliberate stares from people I passed in the foyer.

'What the fuck is everyone looking at?' I quietly mumbled to myself as I exited the lift and strode confidently towards my office.

As I made my way down the corridors more heads seemed to turn in unison towards me. Finally, one kind soul approached with a baby wipe in her outstretched hand. Leaning in, she whispered, 'I think you should go to the ladies.'

'For fuck's sake!' I yelled as I looked at the apparition staring back at me from the mirror. I was covered in huge black spots. The breeze I had felt caress my hair in that dreamy Marilyn Monroe swoosh moment had been harbouring a shovel load of black soot, probably lifted from the train's roof.

I had no choice but to submerge my entire head in water while blowing bubbles and vigorously scrubbing the soot away. As the water drained from the basin, I wrung my hair, tossed it back, and looked into the mirror hoping to see a refreshed, clean version of myself. Instead, I was met by an army of massive, angry red zits marching across my face, which I had temporarily forgotten in my moment of panicked scrubbing. They had broken out a few days earlier and been cleverly concealed by generous lashings of foundation that morning – now that clever zit disguise was somewhere in the plumbing, hurtling towards a water treatment plant. As a result, I spent the rest of the day flashing like a fucking lighthouse.

There were many challenges that came with juggling a demanding career and motherhood. I've always loved the quote, 'Say yes and figure it out when you get there.' It's an inspiring mindset – as long as you consider the impact of your choices on those around you. Trying to balance being a successful professional, a great partner and a present mother is like trying to juggle flaming swords while riding a unicycle... I'm not sure it's possible?

18

Twit for Twat

Everyone looks back on a fashion decision at some point in their life
with regret. You would think that I would have instinctively known that
fad fashion wouldn't end well for me based on my cluster-fucked history.
But by now you would know I am an 'opportunity to shock' addict...

What a day it was – the day a pair of fabulous 'fuck me with the lights on' boots entered my life. I was so besotted that I almost wore them to bed. It took all my patience to hold off their debut until I was certain nothing – including another soot-filled 'swoosh' moment on the London underground – would ruin their grand entrance. But when I finally slipped those boots on, I transformed into a glorious fusion of Britney Spears in her *Oops I did it Again* music video and Madonna belting out *Like a Virgin*. This was my chance to cement my fashionista credentials with the London set.

With these tantalising thoughts filling my head, I stepped from the crowded lift at work, kicking my feet forward in a march reminiscent of stern-faced soldiers strutting through the squares of Pyongyang. Alas, my moment of military precision was cut brutally short. The spaghetti of straps from my rucksack had become entangled between my right ankle and knee, and quicker than you could say fuckmeboots, I was crowd surfing across the floor. I hit the deck with such force that my knees dug into the crappy dark-blue-square-light-blue-square repeated ad-nauseam carpet, tearing up a few squares in the process. I ploughed unceremoniously towards my ultimate stop like an aeroplane crash-landing into a field.

With knees now skinned by carpet burns and my fuck me boots now fucked and missing a top layer of brown leather, I glanced back at the lift wondering what my fellow commuters would do. Would they hold the doors open? Would someone step out to help me? Or would they just pretend they hadn't seen it? Yep. The lift doors pinged closed, and the faces of the occupants disappeared as the green light signalled its onward and upward journey. My fellow citizens of planet earth had made their choice – do the square root of fuck-all – which in hindsight was probably for the best considering I looked like a right dick. I slowly peeled myself off the floor and tried to regain a modicum of composure while dusting myself off.

Rick was one of the world's best bosses. He was a non-judgmental enabler who encouraged my individuality. He allowed me to learn and grow, always pushing me to reach new heights and never making me feel like I was doing it wrong. He was my hero of that decade... and my new Hank.

Hank, you'll remember, was the one who interviewed me when I was an ill-prepared Barbie applying for my first real job. He gave me my big break, telling me never to stop laughing, and to always be myself. He pointed me in the right direction and set me on a path, armed with newfound self-confidence.

So, while Rick may have taken over as my guiding light, Hank's lessons were still very much alive in everything I did. It was like having two mentors – one who helped me build a foundation of self-worth and the other who helped me soar with self-confidence.

Rick was the one who had interviewed me when I presented myself at the job interview dressed like a man. He hadn't said anything at the time, but years later he reminded me by asking, 'I remember you attending the interview dressed as a gangster, what was that all about?'

'I just wanted you to know I could do the job as well as any man,' I replied.

'I could already see that... you didn't need to wear the clothes to make the point. I saw your potential and I wanted you as part of my team,' he said.

Rick never suggested I should change; he supported me to be me through praise and encouragement. My single mother status hadn't fazed him when we first met, nor did he ever bother to ask about my lack of academic qualifications. While he was the ultimate professional and exceptionally talented, he also had a delightful and endearingly quirky streak. One of his little joys was popping into charity shops once a week to add to his collection of ties. Unfortunately, his sartorial skills lagged some way behind his business acumen, and he would bounce into the office wearing some offensive tie wrapped around his neck.

'Oh look, I've just added Versace to my collection!' he would announce jovially as a well-worn, hideous creation – verging on the criminal – bounced about on his stomach.

This scene played out week after week, the only variation being the brand of ties. Christian Dior had his turn, as did Gucci and Yves St Laurent. Ties aside, Rick never lost his composure. He always knew exactly what to say and do – an enormous skill given his unenviable job of running London's ten prisons. And he never used profanities... well, almost never.

His executive assistant, Sandy, had called in sick on the very day he needed fifteen pages of handwritten speech notes to be typed for an important address he was to give to the Treasury in Westminster that evening. Rick approached me and asked if I could set aside my staff officer duties for an hour or two and type his important speech notes. I couldn't refuse, especially as I fancied myself as something of a dab hand at typing. It was probably the most useful thing I'd learnt at school – and only because I saw it as a way to a boy's heart.

I had a crush on a hot teen called Jeff Madden, who was a few years older than me. His brother, Russell, was my age and sat next to me in the typing class. I figured if I could befriend Russell, I'd somehow find my way into Jeff's world and all would be perfect. I never did get to Jeff as his eye was firmly on my friend Mandy, whose boobs were way more impressive than my then pancakes at fourteen. But acquiring typing skills proved to be a more than adequate second prize, and one that would serve me well on this occasion.

'Consider it done,' I assured Rick.

His scribbles were known for being mostly illegible and looked more like they belonged in an ancient book of hieroglyphics than a modern London office. With a bit of deciphering, my fingers danced across the keyboard capturing Rick's impressive writing style and the sage messages he would be sharing with some seriously important people in a few hours. Then I found myself giggling. There was something very funny – and out of character – in one part of the speech. Indeed, my mind couldn't help but picture the audience belly-laughing at his sense of humour.

The following morning, still feeling very proud of my intervention as a touch typist extraordinaire, I ambled over to Rick's office to find him buried in the forest of papers that hit his desk each day. Resplendent in one of his latest charity shop ties, he looked up as I knocked and politely gestured me to come in.

'I just thought I would pop by to hear how last night's speech at the Treasury went?' I asked, eager to hear his take on the evening.

A hint of a smile creased his face, and a small chuckle escaped. 'Yeah, it was good, it was really good... and thanks again for typing up the notes.'

'That's great! It was my pleasure, Boss,' I replied, still basking in my self-appointed typing glory. However, as I made my way to my office, I did think his chuckle was maybe hiding something.

It wasn't long before I heard my role predecessor, Mike, making his way down the corridor, cheerfully greeting colleagues as he went. His voice tapered off as he reached my door and then his head appeared in my doorway.

'Ah, Rick's speech last night was a cracker,' he announced with a grin.

'I believe it was,' I replied proudly. 'I popped by Rick's office a moment ago and he assured me it had gone down well. I knew it would be well-received. He's such a great speaker and a great writer.'

Mike let the silence hang. The pregnant pause grew with each ticking second.

'Okay, so you didn't find anything particularly funny in the notes, then?' he asked, raising an eyebrow.

'Well, there was one really funny bit,' I replied, suppressing a giggle. I detected a slight smirk on Mike's face as he left, but didn't think too much about it. I continued to feel pretty chuffed that everything had gone so smoothly, the praise poured in, and I had played my part in its success.

Two days later and gathered in the boardroom for an executive briefing, the topic inexplicably turned to unintended humour. It was Rick's cue. He leaned forward in his chair at the head of the table, peered over the top of his glasses and scanned the room, ensuring he had everyone's attention.

'Ah, chance humour,' he bellowed. 'You can't beat it.' He paused for effect, letting the anticipation build.

'A few days back when Sandy was off sick, my trusty staff officer stepped in to type up the speech I had to deliver that evening. What I wrote in longhand was...' His voice tapered off and I instinctively braced myself.

'Actually, let me share the evening's unfolding events,' Rick continued. 'Westminster was packed with senior civil servants and politicians. As the Master of Ceremonies, I stood at the podium, looking down at my beautifully typed notes resting on the stand. The audience was nodding along, clearly engaged with my points. Then, I glanced down at my speech and read aloud, "and sometimes that makes me feel like a right..." Whoa, that's not what I wrote! So I told the audience my executive assistant was off ill earlier in the week and my staff officer jumped in to type up my handwritten notes. What I had scribbled was, "and sometimes that makes me feel like a right twit". She, however, has rather interestingly misspelt twit...'

Everyone in the room erupted into laughter. I could feel every eye turn towards me. I had unwittingly landed Rick with a line that read, 'and sometimes that makes me feel like a right twat.'

I'd always prided myself on 'getting shit done', but my ego was a blind spot. I thought I had all the answers. Confidence drove me forward without always asking the right questions. Looking back, I realise that a lack of curiosity hindered both my personal and professional growth. Curiosity isn't just about avoiding mistakes – it's about opening the doors to improve ourselves.

19

freedom

The unconventional role of a prison officer fed my desire to find some semblance of joy in the workplace every day. While prisons are often referred to as a microcosm of society, I've often wondered which part of society mirrors shitting into an origami box. However, one element of prison life was the same both inside and out – the occasional media scrum involving a celebrity.

Professionally, Rick and I were purring along like a well-oiled machine, even when the occasional spanner was tossed into the works by celebrities finding their way into our prisons. As the capital of the United Kingdom, London is not only the place to be, but also the epicenter where celebrities and their fans gather – and of course the world's media is never far behind.

Awash with money and adoration, some celebrities inevitably find themselves in trouble and are packed off to a London prison to either await sentencing on remand or to serve time following their conviction.

There's nothing glamourous about locking up a celebrity. They bring with them a logistical nightmare – not necessarily due to their personal behaviour, but because of the massive media circus that surrounds their incarceration.

In principle, all prisoners should be treated equally, regardless of their fame. It was our responsibility to ensure their wellbeing and reintegrate them into society – ideally, rehabilitated. However, managing celebrity prisoners required us to develop tailored strategies to navigate the inevitable media scramble that would greet their arrival at prison. It was our job to protect them – not only from other prisoners, but also from a misguided staff member who may be eager for an autograph or, worse, their own fleeting moment of fame.

Above all, our greatest fear was having any prisoner die on our watch. In many cases, celebrities were treated as vulnerable prisoners, often placed in segregation for their own safety. The risks were numerous, as other inmates might target them, either out of envy or for blackmail opportunities. Most likely, this would lead to a fellow inmate offering 'protection' – at a price. However, the segregation strategy wasn't without its own challenges, as often, celebrities found themselves next door to some of the more unsavoury characters – like the shit-artist who smeared my beautiful Tag Heuer with his excrement just for entertainment.

Every morning, Rick and I would sift through court appearance lists and the tabloids, scanning for any mention of a celebrity who might be facing charges that day. We'd weigh the odds of them being remanded to one of our facilities and plan accordingly, always bracing for the media storm that would inevitably follow.

'Oh my God, Rick, look who is in a holding cell awaiting court this morning,' I blurted out, spitting coffee over the front page of *The Sun* newspaper.

Sure enough, the celebrity in question arrived at the prison gates later that day.

This time it was George Michael. He had been sentenced to eight weeks for crashing his car under the influence of drugs. He was celebrity royalty, and any photo of him in his standard prison-issue tracksuit would fetch a massive sum from the tabloids. As expected, on the day of his arrival, a platoon of paparazzi swarmed the court, documenting every moment – from the guilty verdict to the transfer from the holding cells to the white armoured van that, under police escort and at high-speed, would deliver him to our prison gates. The paparazzi joined the motorcade, riding pillion on motorbikes while the riders themselves performed kamikaze stunts as they swerved in and out of traffic to draw alongside the van. The photographers on the back leaned over in suicidal poses, with their cameras outstretched in a desperate attempt to capture a glimpse of George.

As the convoy reached the gates, the photographers dismounted, pushing and shoving to get a better position as George remained hidden inside the van. The van backed up to the prison gates and a privacy shield was swiftly rolled into place, allowing George to slip into his new, temporary home, unseen. Without a celebrity plan in place, the situation would have unfolded very differently. We had selected the right team of prison staff to look after the music icon. They had all been through the superstar prisoner circus on many occasions and were not in the least overawed or mesmerised by his arrival.

However, even the best laid plans can go awry. After George Michael was transferred to another prison in a different area of the UK, a prison officer was convicted for leaking confidential information about him. The officer was found guilty of disclosing details about the pop star's life in prison, including sensitive information about his health. Allegedly, she also provided a sketch of the layout of the singer's room, highlighting a large tree outside the prison's perimeter where a photographer was later spotted lurking. In return for her efforts, media reported that she was paid over two thousand pounds. Her actions led to a twelve-month prison sentence and, as a rather fitting comeuppance, she was hit in the face by a urine and faeces 'bomb', presumably thrown by an inmate who was a George Michael fan.

Other celebrities to pass through our doors back then included Blake Fielder-Civil, whose claim to fame at that time was his short-lived marriage to Amy Winehouse.

Another notable guest was Pete Doherty, the singer of *The Libertines* and *Babyshambles,* and once-partner of super model Kate Moss.

Unbeknown to me, my time working alongside Rick, was nearing its end. Having gained valuable first-hand experience in both prisons and probation, I was assigned the daunting task of merging the Prisons' London headquarters and the Probation London headquarters. These two services required very different skill sets, each demanding a distinct approach from their front-line employees. While it wasn't an exact science, it's fair to say that Probation operated in a more nuanced space, focusing on reducing reoffending through partnerships, collaboration, listening and conciliation. On the other hand, the world of Prisons was more black-and-white, its core responsibility being public protection and ensuring that prisoners served their sentences securely.

While the task ahead of me was a natural progression, doubts began to creep in. Imposter syndrome was starting to consume me. Was I really good enough for this?

I had always prided myself on my ability to get things done, but now in this new role, the stakes felt much higher. I found myself questioning whether I was truly prepared for the challenge of merging two distinct cultures. The fear of making the wrong decision – of not being able to bridge the gap between Prisons and Probation services – started to weigh heavily on me. Sure, I had dealt with complex situations before, but this felt different. It wasn't just about navigating high-profile cases; it was about driving systemic change. The responsibility was daunting, and to be honest, I felt a deep unease about whether I was truly up to the task. What if I'm not enough for this? The fear of failure kept gnawing at me, reminding me of just how much was riding on my ability to get this right.

While my experience with the intricacies of celebrity prisoners had certainly sharpened my problem-solving skills, merging the Prison and Probation divisions was proving to be my toughest challenge yet. I did have some tools in my kit, though – skills like building relationships and communicating effectively, which had been honed over years of navigating complex situations. But even with those skills, the pressure felt overwhelming.

One standout moment during this time, when I really had to step up, was when I was tasked with negotiating eight rioting women down off the prison roof.

These women had decided a rooftop protest was the best way to air their grievances about food and conditions in custody. Normally, rooftop protests were uncomfortable, short-lived affairs – wet, cold roofs weren't exactly ideal venues for an extended protest. But not that day. The sun was shining, temperatures were in the high twenties, and it felt more like a summer garden party than a standoff.

The women were living it up – suntan lotion, no clothes – and the national media choppers circling overhead and tabloid photographers captured titillating shots that made for interesting headlines. Their notoriety grew daily, turning the situation into pure theatre unfortunately.

Meanwhile, prisoners in the cells immediately below showed their solidarity by fashioning makeshift ropes from torn-up bed linens, using them to send food and drink up to the protestors, ensuring their resistance didn't falter due to hunger or thirst.

I'd learnt never to underestimate the ingenuity of women, especially when they had time on their hands. As part of the prison's Women in Education program, we had taught the women origami. So naturally, they put those skills to work by making 'shit box bombs' from newspapers. These weren't your typical gently lowered paper creations. No, these bombs were launched with great enthusiasm – and aimed directly at me, the negotiator. Suddenly, I found myself dodging and weaving like a character in *Donkey Kong*, ducking and swerving as projectiles came flying at me. And of course, the women on the roof, along with the watching prisoners below, cheered with delight every time one of their shots hit its mark. I was soon covered with various splashes of shit. It was that day I learnt the oddly useless fact that everyone's shit is a different colour. Judging by the various shades of brown splattered across my white shirt, I'd guesstimate I was wearing at least three different humans contributions.

Eventually, the UK's notoriously fickle weather played its hand. The clouds rolled in, the temperatures dipped, and with it the novelty of the protest wore off. The prisoners calmly descended from the roof, bringing the impromptu standoff to an end. Normally, I might have felt a sense of self-doubt, as it could have been interpreted as a failure of negotiation. After all, when prisoners come down from a roof due to bad weather, it's easy to assume that the negotiator had no part in it. But, in these situations, a successful outcome is one where no one gets hurt, and a peaceful resolution is achieved – whatever form that might take. The role of the negotiator is to keep the conversation going, gather as much information as possible, and help everyone to stay safe.

Merging the two worlds of Prisons and Probation was no easy feat. It felt like I was wading through a vat of tar – slow, sticky, and frustrating – and much as I tried not to, I rattled a few cages along the way. The cultures between the two organisations were so different that I often felt like I was trying to put a square peg into round hole. The creation of one Offender Management Service likely sparked a sense of identity loss and uncertainty on both sides, leaving many questioning, including me, where they belonged.

The Probation team had swish offices with spectacular views across the River Thames, while the Prison folk occupied more... shall we say, sombre digs – the kind with air-filtration systems so ancient they were rumoured to be part of a World War II experiment to keep germs circulating. I couldn't help but envy the views of the river my newest colleagues enjoyed as I battled with recycled flu particles – probably from someone sneezing their way around an office five storeys above and making me sick every couple of weeks. Still, it became part of the process – a constant reminder that amid change, there would always be hurdles, and you just had to keep pushing forward.

As the merger focused on creating a more seamless criminal justice system, it wasn't long before our friends on the Thames were informed that they'd be relocating to join us Prison people in our more utilitarian surroundings. Needless to say, the news was met with a mix of disappointment and frustration. For those leaving behind their impressive offices, the move was understandably less than appealing. For those staying in the sombre digs, it was disappointing news that the view and air-conditioning wasn't about to significantly improve.

For me, the antidote for the stress of the merger came from a new addition to my responsibilities – anti-corruption and counterterrorism.

This was my James Bond moment – going through the rigorous security clearances, being trained in investigative techniques, learning how to authorise secret-squirrel surveillance and managing informants, or a 'grass' in street parlance. The experience was as eye-opening as it was occasionally hilarious. I'd love to tell you some of the stories... but I'd have to kill you if I did.

Following the London bombings in July 2005, the focus on counterterrorism intensified the world over. Our division established a Counter Terrorism Task Force in partnership with the Metropolitan Police to tackle the growing threat of radicalisation and violent extremism behind bars. I was honoured to be asked to manage this crucial initiative for London, especially given my limited experience in this area.

My own experience with terrorism in the prison system up until that point had been limited to having stepped foot in the same jail as prisoner Richard Reid, the infamous 'shoe bomber', who had been incarcerated in the 1990s. Reid's journey from petty thief to *al-Qaeda* operative highlighted how quickly the landscape of terrorism was evolving. We simply didn't know what we didn't know.

Reid had concocted a plan to detonate explosives hidden in his shoes while flying from Paris to Miami. Thankfully, the plot failed when the explosive didn't detonate, likely due to a combination of soaked shoes from rainy weather in Paris and the delayed departure of his flight, which caused his foot perspiration to dampen the fuse. I like to think that Paris's litter of chewing gum and dog shit played a role too – though that detail was omitted from the reports.

After a brief scuffle with flight attendants, Reid was subdued by fellow passengers, tranquillised by a doctor on board, and arrested when the plane made an emergency landing in Boston. He is now serving a life sentence in the US.

Of course, not all prisoners are bad apples. During my time in the system, I encountered many people who were simply down on their luck or in need of a second chance. Sometimes, people just need a break or a guardian angel – much like Hank had been for me.

> *I wore an invisible badge of doubt that made me feel like an imposter. I let it question my abilities and make me wonder whether I was truly capable of handling the challenges that came my way. The lesson? Don't measure your worth by the fear in your mind. Trust that you're where you are because you belong.*

20

fat Controller

The four-hour commute each day was becoming a royal pain in my arse, and it was clear something needed to change. Cue crisis number thirteen thousand nine hundred and eleven...

The Global Financial Crisis of 2007/08 sent shockwaves around the world. Governments everywhere, including those in Westminster, scrambled to find ways to cut costs. Outsourcing quickly became the buzzword of the day. One evening, while heading home from work, the penny dropped for me. Tired, slightly dishevelled and among squillions of automated commuters, I glanced around the sea of heads buried in newspapers, all absorbed in the day's grim news.

'With the government tightening its belt, and me wanting to take the next step in my career, I reckon I need to get a better understanding of the private sector and the commercial world,' I suggested to LNT as we took in more bleak economic updates on the TV.

He nodded in that way LNT does – just enough to signal agreement, but not with the enthusiasm that would imply it was a fucking brilliant idea. Still, I felt the resolution from inside me – I'd add a few commercial strings to my bow.

Serendipity had been a constant companion throughout my career, and it made its presence felt once again a few weeks later when I came across an advert placed by a former boss, Alfie. At the time, he had taken on responsibility for a large region in the UK, which included several private prisons. The ad was for a Controller – essentially a senior contract manager in British government parlance – nominated by the Home Secretary to oversee the private contractors delivering services to the government.

Alfie and I had worked together in London, and I knew him as a seasoned professional for whom I had immense respect. He was a bit of a maverick, his free spirit and bold unorthodoxy especially apparent in how he saw risk – not as a threat, but as an opportunity. His intellect was sharp, and he had little tolerance for grey areas or fools. With Alfie, you always knew exactly where you stood, and I was fortunate that he didn't consider me a fool. As a result, I knew I had earned a place on the good side of his ledger, which eased any reservations I might have had about applying to work for him again.

I was bubbling with excitement at the prospect of the role and the power it offered the successful candidate. With my experience and Alfie knowing exactly what he would get from me, I breezed through the interview process and secured the position. The downside was bidding farewell to Rick and the London crowd, as the job required a move to the centre of England. But the upside was immense – it meant I could say hello to a whole new life, one that would fulfil my materialistic dreams. My heart was set on building the perfect life to match what I was certain would be the perfect job, marking my successful entrée into the commercial world.

We sold our comfortable double-storey home in Oxfordshire and bought a triple-storey, six-bedroomed mansion in a village close to my new office. Why? Because... I'd never done it before, and I wanted to. In my relentless drive to outdo myself, I stretched my limits to grasp the next big thing. The fact that the third floor, complete with two bedrooms with en-suite bathrooms, was hardly used during the twenty-two months we called it home mattered not. It was my mini castle, the next step into my fairy-tale world.

My version of the perfect life also demanded the perfect body. A constant reminder of this prerequisite being the little model of The Fat Controller from *Thomas the Tank Engine* that stared at me from its strategically placed spot on my desk. I was acutely aware of the need to watch my weight, lest I balloon and end up saddled with a cruel nickname that would mirror my ridiculous Controller title.

My weight loss regimen was intense. I signed up for *Weight Watchers,* swapped full cream milk for some bland, light shite, and tackled my Coke addiction the same way – no, I'm not talking about cocaine. Tut-Tut. I'm referring to switching from the sugar-loaded variety to the diet alternative. I even managed to limit myself to just one takeaway a week. The results were brilliant. In no time I'd shed nearly thirty pounds and regained a surge of energy.

Feeling great and looking good, I pranced around the bedroom taking in everything the floor-to-ceiling mirror reflected at me. But 'good' was not enough. 'Damn you, mirror,' I grumbled at the sheet of reflective glass. 'I won't allow perfection to escape me a moment longer.' It was my tits that let the side down. Their saggy sadness needed to make way for ones that stood proud and to attention. New boobs, new life, blah, blah... all for self-gratification, of course. LNT however, couldn't have cared less. He showed his usual indifference with a casual, barely-there nod when I shared my decision.

Driven by my work ethic, I tackled this enhancement project without taking a single day off. I had the procedure on a Friday afternoon and was back at work by Monday, my baggy clothes cleverly hiding the swelling until it subsided. I was so good at concealing it that no one at work was any the wiser.

The first week of recovery required a bit of scaffolding to keep me upright and let me sleep in a chair without squashing my new puppies beyond recognition. As I progressed to the bedroom, I couldn't risk sharing a bed with LNT. I was haunted by the thought of him accidentally rolling over and crushing one of them so badly that the stitches would tear and the nipple would be sheared clean off. The nightmare leaving me staring down in horror at a deep crevice, through a transparent silicone implant, at my own beating heart.

The temporary solitary confinement on the third floor was one of my more sensible decisions. My brand-new red BMW now adorning my driveway made me feel even better, a sense of worthiness washing over me.

I did experience a brief moment of doubt amidst all this opulence when Amy, approaching two years old, transitioned from her cot to a bed. Shit, what would happen if this poor child, now free from the safety of her cot, fell out of bed in the middle of the night? I imagined her rolling towards the door at such an angle that she slipped through and turned left, heading towards the spiral staircase connecting the three floors, only to be bounced down to the cold, hard hallway floor, dozens of feet below. Though wildly improbable, this thought gripped me with a momentary wave of fear. But just as quickly, it was snuffed out by the sight of the red BMW parked on the herringbone-patterned red brick driveway. My heart swelled with joy once more. Yes, I had the perfect life...

The commercially-oriented environment brought daily challenges and excitement as I worked long hours to master overseeing the numerous contracts we had with the private companies running outsourced prisons. It was my responsibility to ensure they delivered on their promise to provide services more cost-effectively, without cutting corners. These companies were tasked with making sure everything was available when needed, from food in the kitchens to soap in the showers.

I became a sponge, absorbing all the knowledge I could as I embarked on this epic learning journey. It was a tough gig, full of sharp turns, most of which I navigated smoothly, helped along by a spanking red BMW and a new pair of tits.

I quickly became damn good at my job and found myself wielding more clout than ever before. Thanks to the powers delegated to me by the Home Secretary, I could approve the release of prisoners, suspend officers, authorise covert surveillance, and during major incidents, represent the British government as a commander in the incident command suite. But the core of my role was to monitor the commercial contract delivery. These private businesses were obviously in it to make money. I, as the representative of the British government, was there to ensure there was no shortfall in the expected care for prisoners. It was a scenario fraught with potential conflict, and before long, I learned I was secretly known as 'Vinegar Tits', a nod to the acerbic senior prison officer from the Australian television drama *Prisoner*. The character who was notoriously harsh and nearly impossible to warm to. I took it as part of the job and didn't flinch in my resolve to make sure contract delivery was on point. My mantra was simple: every prisoner had to be treated respectfully, and I would do everything I could to see to it that, fairness and consistency would be mandatory on my watch.

Unsavoury moments came and went, with most being defused and resolved before they became untenable. One however, stood out. Believe it or not, I was warned while walking down the high street to relent on a particular issue or I would be: 'Crushed like a bug!' I was left feeling bemused by the comment. As they scuttled away, much like a sniper would – 'nothing to see here...' – I noticed something strange; each step they took was accompanied by a loud, rhythmic 'tap tap' sound. I looked down, expecting to see toes dangling over the front of their shoes, with long brittle toenails scraping the pavement. But no – oddly, they were wearing closed toe shoes. I can only assume the soles of the shoes had evolved to match their habitat...

Liz's presence was altogether different. As my new second-in-command, she was wonderfully calm, highly efficient and astute. She was able to find humour even in the darkest of moments and often had me in stitches with her wickedly idiosyncratic take on life. Positioned a few feet away from me, Liz was ordering us both a coffee at a mobile refreshment van. As the tap-tap duet of the Anubis figures faded into the distance, I heard the distinctive sniggering of Liz.

'Don't tell me that just fucking happened?' she asked incredulously.

'Indeed it did,' I replied, still smirking at the encounter, but feeling a lot better knowing Liz had heard it. Our dissection of the crazy episode, looking at it from every angle and finding humour in the image of me being crushed like a bug, really warmed me to Liz.

We clicked that day and quickly became a strong team. Our partnership developed an uncanny telepathic connection, making us perfect work partners. We reached a point where we knew exactly what the other was thinking – none more so than the day a man named Graham, rolled into work looking like he'd taken a wrong turn on his way to an Elvis Lookalike Convention. Deep in the throes of his mid-life crisis, he'd dyed his prematurely grey hair jet black. With his short stature, it gave him a comically cheap resemblance to 'The King' – or at least, that's what he thought...

Later that morning as Liz and I shared project details with Graham in my office, he leaned forward over the meeting table to stress a point. 'Let me just say...'

Before he could finish the sentence, I was unable to stop my interjecting, mumbling, 'Ah, hah hah...'

Graham straightened his tie thinking it was an answer in the affirmative, even though the question hadn't been asked yet. Liz, however, knew precisely what I was playing at and gave me a wide-eyed look. I continued my rather juvenile game, and Graham's many suggestions elicited a series of increasingly louder, 'Ah hah hah...' responses from me.

The combination of my childish joke soaring right over Graham's head soon had Liz 'all shook up... ah hah hah...' She lost the battle to retain her composure and was seconds away from wetting herself. She pursed her lips, allowing only a few soft fart-like noises to escape. Her face turned red as she shuffled uncomfortably in her chair, crossing her legs then swinging them over in the opposite direction and crossing them still tighter, before dashing to the ladies' room. By the time she returned, Elvis had left the office... if not the building.

Elvis remained nonplussed for many months until I let my little private joke slip during a creative abrasion session (aka disagreement). He grew increasingly frustrated with our deadlock and announced that he would take a break and go for a walk to clear his thoughts – hoping it would help him reach a resolution.

'And don't wear open-toed shoes to work anymore, it is a health and safety risk,' he snapped as he departed.

'Sure thing, Elvis,' I replied, my tone a little teenager like. I was already frustrated after an exhausting session in which little progress had been made. Whatever possessed me to say it, the secret was out, and I was mortified. The only silver lining was that poor Elvis never dyed his hair again. He was a good guy, doing a good job. Our roles on opposite sides of the fence meant that there would always be competitive tension between us. But the key to achieving the shared goal of keeping people safely in custody and rehabilitating them was to work as a partnership – and always shake hands at the end of each debate – which we did well.

The silliness between Liz and I often extended beyond the office, resulting in work-related walkabouts as we hunted for anything that could brighten our day. Liz, ever the persuasive one, managed to convince me to have false eyelashes glued to my eyelids just a day before LNT and I were due to fly off for a short holiday in Mauritius. The procedure was done by her local beautician, and at first, they looked fantastic – all neatly lined up and securely in place. That is, until halfway through the flight, high above the Indian Ocean, I absentmindedly scratched an itchy eye. To my horror, my hand was filled with a lump of limp lashes. With half of them gone and the other half unnaturally long, I turned to LNT, desperately seeking reassurance that it wasn't as bad as it felt. The customary nod came, but I knew as I walked up to the poor chap at Passport Control, that I looked like a prize wanker. I called Liz to demand a complimentary appointment with her beautician as soon as I got back to the UK, but she was unable to speak such were her fits of laughter. She did make the appointment for me, and in between apologetic words from the beautician, I learnt that the dry airplane air had likely rendered the glue ineffective – no shit Sherlock!

Another of Liz's persuasive pearlers convinced me that the best way to remove old, dry and hard heel skin was to have a school of fish munch on the offending foot. As expected, it didn't work, and I walked away more convinced than ever that only a shoal of fucking piranhas could replace the trusty old foot file.

Sadly, our fun and games, and the very good work we did together to ensure the contractors kept their end of the bargain, would soon be over.

As we walked through the prison grounds late one summer afternoon, Liz stopped abruptly and nervously announced that she had something important to tell me.

'Don't tell me,' I said as our innate telepathy took over, 'you're pregnant.'

We held each other's hands, and I squeezed hers tightly. She was over the moon with her new mum-to-be status, and I was genuinely happy for her. But the realisation that our fun work time was about to end hit us both hard, and before we knew it, we were hugging each other tightly.

'What about me, you selfish twat?' I blurted out trying to lighten the mood as we stood there both cry-laughing.

The next morning, serendipity struck again. My world took an unexpected turn when I opened my emails to find an invitation via LinkedIn asking me to consider applying for an executive position in the South Australian Prison Service.

'Look at this scammer trying to get my details,' I said, pushing my mobile phone under LNT's nose as he lay spread out on the living room sofa watching the early edition of Sky News.

'Why don't you Google him before jumping to conclusions?' he suggested in his annoyingly mature way. I took his advice and returned to tell him that the guy who had contacted me was very real according to Google.

'Are you up for it?' I asked.

'I'm up for it,' LNT replied.

That was it. The decision was made. I drove the thirty miles to work amazed at how little thought we had given it. I didn't even know where Adelaide was, as my knowledge of Australian geography was limited to Sydney and its Opera House, along with some vast, hot and dusty place the locals called The Outback. More to the point, I didn't care. Adelaide was somewhere in Australia, and the sun shone across the entire country, unlike the fleeting little bursts of sunshine we got in the UK. That was enough for me. My near-perfect world would be completely perfect with a regular injection of sunshine.

'I reckon I could be applying for a job in Australia,' I excitedly told Liz the moment I got to work.

'That's rebound that is, and I have to say an extreme reaction to me taking six-months' maternity leave,' Liz responded, tongue in cheek. 'What's the job, and what do you know about Australia or where you'll be based? It's a bloody gigantic country!' Liz continued, not unreasonably.

'I don't really know,' I admitted.

'You're fucking mad enough to do it, you are,' Liz declared.

I could only nod my head. 'Ab-sah-fucking-loot-ly...'

As I bid farewell to this chapter of my life, I came to realise that Hank was right; laughter was an invaluable tool for lightening the load when life gets heavy. It's the thread that bonds us with others. What I hadn't fully understood however, is that to truly move forward – to cross the ocean – I would have to let go of the comfort of the shore.

21

Eyes on the Prize

I would be crap in I'm a Celebrity... Get Me Out of Here – not just because I'm not famous, but because I'm useless when it comes to non-British food. There I was, in a foreign restaurant, about to have a dalliance with a dinner whose face was still very much intact and staring right back at me, begging for mercy. A little context is needed here – if my dinner could talk, it would've been saying, 'You're out of your depth.'

I rushed home that evening, taking a deep breath as I sat with a poker straight back in my gingham cloth director's chair at my study desk. Eagerly, I typed a simple 'yes, I'm interested' email and clicked send. As it zipped off to Australia, I dared to dream that it would result in a new and exciting life. I hadn't had much time to reflect before receiving a late-night reply – thanking me for my interest and requesting that I complete the official application and attach my CV.

'Shit!' I muttered, my mind racing at the thought of writing a CV.

I was a Haverhill girl who had ended up, almost by chance, in the Prison Service, moving from one promotion to the next. It was my performance record rather than some wordy document that did the talking. I couldn't help but feel a little inadequate, as there wasn't much to showcase in my CV – or so I thought... I couldn't impress them with an Oxford or Cambridge degree, not even a diploma from some lesser-known regional polytechnic. My best bet was to surreptitiously embed the eye-catching 'Oxford' and 'Cambridge' in the text, though any reader with a modicum of nous would immediately detect my association with these alluring names was only due to living near them at some time.

I am sure I occasionally, well, at least once, set foot on both campuses so perhaps I could indulge in a little creative licence? But after some thought, I realised the Oxbridge references wouldn't cut it. In frustration, I tore up my first draft. I started over... and over again, until I finally had what I believed was a worthy résumé. When I clicked on the 'send attachment' button, I knew my application lacked creativity and I hadn't done a particularly flash job at selling myself, but at least it was done.

With a feeling of relief, a week later, I received a positive reply asking me to make myself available for a telephone interview with a panel of senior executives. We were now entering the big league. Being a bit obsessive, I vowed to do everything in my power to secure my slice of sunshine on the other side of the world.

I started by diving deep into research on South Australia and dug into the history of the Australian penal system, tracing its roots back to 1788, when the first Irish petty criminal arrived, having stolen a loaf of bread. As I uncovered valuable tidbits, I jotted them down on Post-it notes and plastered them across my walls. Every time I walked by them while going about domestic chores, I recited the key messages they held.

When the phone rang at the agreed time that late summer evening, I felt in total control. My answers were locked in my head and if stress blocked their instant recall, I knew precisely where to find the relevant note. My performance was a far cry from the knob I had once subjected dear old Hank to all those years before.

Gut instinct told me I had nailed the interview. This was confirmed a few days later when I was invited to travel to Singapore for a second round of interviews, where I would meet the decision-makers face to face. Fair enough, I thought, they don't know me from Eve... I could have been mad, bad, or even both. Maybe they just wanted to make sure I didn't show up dressed like a punk rocker, with a Mohican hairstyle or huge holes in my earlobes!

When my flight reservation email arrived, I noticed that I had been booked into a different hotel from the interviewing crew. I figured that was in case I turned out to be a complete goose, they could just tell me how nice it had been to meet me, wish me a safe and enjoyable trip home, and avoid any embarrassing encounters at reception the next morning when checking out.

The first meeting was an informal breakfast at their hotel with two of the organisation's executives, presumably sent ahead as the vanguard to suss me out. True to their Aussie nature in a tropical setting, both strolled in looking more like holidaymakers, dressed in T-shirts, shorts, and thongs. This was in stark contrast to the professional black pinstriped suit I had carefully selected for the occasion. But it must have gone well, as one of them called me 'mate' when saying farewell. I took that as a sign that we were already pals after just one coffee. The invitation to join them for dinner at a riverside Singaporean restaurant further reinforced my sense of success.

'It's within your grasp,' I told myself. 'Don't fuck it up by getting lost on your way to the restaurant – or worse still, going to the wrong one.'

Google maps on mobile phones wasn't widely used at this point, so I spent the afternoon studying visitor guides to Singapore while lapping up the heat and sunshine by the hotel pool. I marked the route from my hotel to the restaurant with a fluorescent pink highlighter and calculated how long the walk would take. Following my carefully planned directions, I arrived at the restaurant overlooking the river, where I settled in to await my interrogators. To pass the time, I studied the menu, which was filled with exotic dishes made from critters I had never heard of. I even practiced pronouncing their names to try to avoid butchering the poor creatures again when it was time to order.

I couldn't help but curse my distinctly British upbringing, where 'exotic' food didn't go much further than Yorkshire Pudding smothered in gravy. The familiar stirrings of my Haverhill roots began to rise, but before I could get too flustered by all this posh stuff encircling me, my attention was drawn to a cheery voice.

'G'day!' My two hosts had arrived, looking completely at ease in the restaurant and with its fare. They discussed the various dishes and offered recommendations. The male interrogator scanned the abundant wine list for a few seconds before handing it to me.

'There are some top tipples here, whaddaya fancy?' he asked.

Top tipples, whaddaya... I wondered if he had swallowed a bollock? What the fuck was he talking about? I guessed he must be asking me what I wanted to drink. My sommelier skills were limited to the free plonk served by the jug in Turkey – stuff so near flammable that it didn't even have a name. Fearing I could easily pick something ridiculous if I made a blind stab at the wine list, I thought it best to politely suggest that he ordered something for me.

'My wine experience is mostly French and Italian varietals, but since I'm in the company of Australians, I think it's only fitting I try your wine,' I said, putting as much sincerity into my voice as I could muster.

It worked. He selected a bottle from South Australia, and as we waited for it to arrive, the next challenge presented itself – what to choose to eat. Gripped by the white-knuckle fear that comes whenever I feel out of my depth, I reminded myself that I was there for a reason. I needed to win them over, land the job, and add sunshine to my life. I had to at least appear confident and somewhat knowledgeable about the mystifying menu.

Taking a deep breath, I sipped my chilled Adelaide Hills sauvignon blanc and briefly considered a bullshit response along the lines of describing it as 'a bouquet bursting with intense tropical fruit characters, offset by zesty acidity', but I sensibly opted for a more muted reply.

'Hmmm, nice choice...' I said, my eyes quickly returning to the menu, where mercifully, something familiar caught my eye. Squid. More precisely, sweet and sour baby sesame squid. The small print added that it was crispy, which sent my confidence levels skywards as I pictured something not dissimilar to the fare dished up at your typical Brighton beachfront chippy.

It arrived in a large white bowl and smelled like a fishing boat accident that had occurred seven hot days earlier. It was filled to the brim with scores of baby squid that had clearly been hurled alive into a pan of boiling oil only to emerge as rigid statues. The eyes of these poor creatures were where they ought to be, but the tentacles were curled up over their heads as if they knew they were doomed to eternal purgatory. And it wasn't a dainty *cordon bleu* serve either; there was enough there to make a hearty meal for a lumberjack after a gruelling day of tree chopping.

'Would anyone like to try some of my squid? It looks delicious,' I volunteered, my voice breaking with forced enthusiasm.

My offer was knocked back with a consensual alacrity that suggested they had been there before and knew to steer clear of this dish. My only escape route was to eat it and keep reminding myself of the bigger prize. It took a serious effort to get the first crusty squid down my throat. It felt like trying to swallow a grappling hook and I felt my nostrils flare like an enraged bull. I again reminded myself how badly I wanted the job and instructed my brain – and oesophagus – to toughen the fuck up.

I painfully picked my way through the dish. 'Take it for the team, take it for the fucking team...' I silently commanded, battling to keep my facial expressions from exposing the sheer horror I was experiencing.

Thankfully, the rest of the evening seemed to go a lot better, with cordial conversation making for a relaxed and enjoyable night. I felt good about my chances, though I couldn't shake the worry that the squid episode might have been observed and could work against me. Would my hosts think that if this Pommy Sheila couldn't eat some baby critters, what chance did she have of surviving in Australia?

When I got back to my hotel, I still felt utterly violated by the squid and immediately called LNT, demanding that he appreciate the horror of what I'd been through.

'I just came back from a scary restaurant where I had to eat an entire fisherman's catch of baby squid that had been cooked alive!' I wailed. 'I could feel every squid in the sea judging me as I ate a family member with its eyes looking at me and its arms in the air begging for mercy.'

'Well, did you eat them all?' LNT asked, his response as empathetic as a brick wall.

'I gave a sterling performance by getting through half of it,' I shot back, incredulity rising.

'Only half?' he jibed.

'It was a fucking huge portion and it was hurting my throat! Don't make me feel worse than I already do!'

The next morning, with images of eyes and suction cups still haunting me, I sat down for a one-on-one breakfast with the big boss. He told me I had made a favourable impression and that everything in my CV had checked out. Casual as anything, he slid a piece of paper across the table, saying it was a contract and he hoped I would sign it because he really wanted me to fill the position. I glanced at the salary, which was more than I had ever earned before. Instead of showering him with grateful kisses and thanking him profusely, the streetwise kid in me shot back, 'Hmmmm... I think we need to negotiate the package.'

Where the fuck did that come from? Here I was, being offered an enormous salary in a sun-drenched country and I was haggling! 'Add ten thousand dollars to the figure and you have a deal,' I said with all the boldness I could muster, channelling my inner Del Boy in *Only Fools and Horses*. He didn't flinch. He stretched out a hand and confirmed we had a deal.

As it was the middle of the night in the UK and I didn't want to wake LNT, I headed back to my room, changed into casual clothes, threw a backpack over my shoulders, and set off to spend the rest of the day blissfully strolling the streets of Singapore. My treat to myself was to be a tourist for the day – far from the responsibilities of being a life partner and mother, filled with the youthful aura that only sheer independence can bring. Even the thought of possibly sacrificing my stable life in the UK for something that might go completely pear-shaped in a distant land couldn't dull my sense of exhilaration.

'Sod it, we are dead a long time,' I said out loud as I strolled through one of Singapore's many beautiful parks. I wasn't going to die with a 'what-if' hanging over my head. Surely, the worst that could happen is I'd lose some money on a disastrous family relocation.

With my mind made up, and any concern for LNT and his need for sleep forgotten, I cut my tourist trek short and headed back to the hotel to call him with the news. 'There are two envelopes on the microwave,' I instructed. 'One is addressed to my employer – it's my resignation letter. I need you to post it today.'

I could practically hear him shaking on the other end of the phone, stunned by my decisiveness. 'The other envelope is for you. You need to sign it and post it. And one more thing – call the real estate agent and put the house on the market.'

I hung up the phone, kicked my sandals off, and stretched out on the hotel bed. Yes, I was still suffering from post-traumatic squid syndrome, which was likely clouding my judgement, but I felt invincible!

Life rarely hands out neatly tied packages with bows on top. The job offer from the other side of the world and the bowl of squid both came with a side of existential crisis. But here's the thing: I had to dive right in and trust I'd figure it out when I got there. Sometimes you just have to leap, even if you're not sure what you're going to land on!

22

The Whinging Pom

Planning a move to the other side of the world sounds like the start of
an exciting adventure, right? Well, it's all fun and games until you're
knee-deep in panic, and have an overwhelming sense of 'What the hell
have I done?'

I thought I had it all figured out. We'd land in Australia, suitcases in
hand, and our stuff would follow shortly after, ready for our shiny new
life. What I didn't factor in was the small detail of grieving the life I was
leaving behind – because apparently, emotional breakdowns don't make
it into the relocation brochure.

By late September 2011, just days after returning from Singapore,
our house was sold. Thankfully, the settlement allowed us to stay until
early December, which felt like plenty of time. I envisioned a smooth
and leisurely process: packing up our things, arranging for the freight
company to ship our belongings down to Southampton, and then off to
Port Adelaide, Australia. We'd fly out in mid-December and upon arrival
find our household goods waiting for us. We'd settle into our new home,
start our new jobs and before we knew it, we'd be true blue Aussies.

I worked through my notice period and soon enough, the day
arrived for our household goods to be collected. I watched with a mix
of excitement and apprehension as the truck pulled away, our worldly
possessions locked in a container headed for its six-to-twelve-week

journey. It was a leap into the unknown and I hoped we'd land on soft ground.

Gloominess began to set in as the days of waiting for our visas stretched into weeks. I started to face the harsh truth that there was no guarantee that we would get the approvals we needed. We'd taken a massive punt – quitting our jobs, selling our home and shipping our possessions off to Australia. In moments of quiet solitude, I found myself mulling over the Australian migration points system, wondering how we'd measure up against the critical criteria like age, qualifications, and financial standing. I also wrestled with the fact that I'd recently turned forty – the cut-off age for certain visas – and the reality that neither LNT nor I had a tertiary qualification to boost our scores.

After several weeks of waiting, I convinced myself that our chances of being granted a visa were hanging by a thread. But I clung to the small comforts – we had money in the bank and the authorities knew that, so even if everything did turn to shit, we wouldn't be a burden on the Australian taxpayer. Plus, I was an executive with a unique skillset – one that couldn't be learnt from a book – so I ticked the skilled migrant box.

The seemingly endless waiting was taking its toll, turning what should have been an exciting time into a stress fest. I found myself emailing our case officer almost daily with a polite but desperate, 'Any news?' I imagined her in an office somewhere deep within the corridors of Canberra's migration offices, buried under a mountain of paperwork, each file a source of her suffering. She showed remarkable patience in her replies.

'No, sorry, nothing yet, all in due process. I will inform you immediately when I get word...' she would invariably say.

I couldn't help but wonder if 'in due process' was code for, 'Piss off and leave me alone. If you don't, I'll get a restraining order against you motherfucker.' Despite this, I kept firing off my two-word emails, my anxiety mounting as October became November and November became

December. The stress was compounded when we moved to my parents for a few days before imposing ourselves on LNT's father.

'It's just for a couple of weeks,' we assured him, though I had my doubts.

One chilly morning, just days before Christmas, I turned to LNT and said, 'It's not happening this year. It's summer down there. Our case officer will shut down her computer on Christmas Eve, head off for her holidays and probably won't be back at work until after Australia Day on 26 January.'

As the most laid-back person on the planet, LNT was my emotional barometer. When I started noticing his usual calm demeanour shifting and a few subtle signs of unease creeping in, I felt it too, and my own hope began to waver even more. My stress reached such ridiculous levels that I was now sleeping with the fired-up laptop on my bedside table and one ear tuned in for the ping that announced the arrival of an incoming email. Each ping sent me bolting upright within milliseconds. On more than one occasion, I found myself getting up in the middle of the night, brewing a cup of tea, and sitting at the kitchen table staring at my laptop screen, literally praying for that one email.

Then it happened. Just before four o'clock in the morning on Christmas Eve (which, in Canberra was around three on Christmas Eve afternoon), my laptop pinged. A sense of cautious optimism bubbled up, and I took a deep breath before clicking open the email. I read the first few lines slowly, then reread them to make sure I hadn't misinterpreted them.

Are you ready??? Drum roll... it gives me great pleasure to inform you that with the powers vested in me, I hereby grant you your permanent residency in Australia...

That was all I needed to read. I leaned back in my chair and looked up to the ceiling and whispered, 'Thank you.'

I imagined our dear case officer had been about to leave the office and head for some celebratory Christmas drinks. I could almost see her pausing then thinking she had better just shoot this email off before she got the hell out of there for the Christmas break. I never heard from her again, but I hope she knew she'd gifted us the best Christmas present ever.

I rushed upstairs, shook LNT awake, and together we had a good cry.

Christmas Day felt odd. There were no presents being handed out, just three suitcases packed with essentials for our new life in Australia. Amy had to make do with a few cheap disposable gifts that were nonetheless welcomed by the then four-year-old.

With our flight booked for December 28th, the next challenge was to rid ourselves of our almost new cars in the span of a few short days. This meant taking a massive loss on both vehicles and flogging them for what felt like pennies to a car auctioneer shark who, no doubt, retired comfortably from the profit made from them. And that was it, all the material things that once tied us to our old lives in the UK were gone, leaving only the emotional goodbyes to family and close friends before we boarded the plane to the unknown.

The toughest moment of all the farewells came when I said goodbye to my boy, James. My constant, wise young man who had taught me more than I could ever have imagined. As we stood in the bustling chaos of Heathrow Airport, he pulled me close and said with such conviction, 'Go, Mum. You've given me the best childhood ever and it's time to give my little sister the best one too. You are making the right choice. Australia is a safer place to raise her than the UK.'

The words hit me like a tsunami and tears streamed down my face and into my packet of cheesy wotsits. With a heart full of emotions, I trudged through customs and immigration towards the second half of my life.

It wasn't until we were seated on the plane and taxiing for take-off that I was finally able to place my migratory experience into its rightful slot in the greater scheme of things. I took solace by reminding myself that while millions of refugees and asylum seekers were forced to flee unspeakable horrors every year, the only real horror I was leaving behind was *Coronation Street* and around three hundred and twenty days of relentless greyness and drizzle – the grizzle us locals had called it.

Twenty-four hours later, jetlagged and disoriented, we emerged from Adelaide Airport straight into a forty-five-degree Celsius heatwave. The first thing I did was look up at huge blue skies and inhale the dry, unfamiliar air, feeling both the warmth of the sun and the unfamiliarity of a new stage in life unfolding.

'Fuck it's hot,' I wailed to LNT in a classic Whinging Pom tone. 'This is not the Promised Land I had in mind. I want sunshine, but not of the Armageddon variety.' I squinted up at the blazing sky and questioned why the lush, green meadows of England had been replaced by brittle brown grass, the kind that felt like it belonged to a dusty desert, not a welcoming new home.

LNT however, was in a different world altogether. He stepped off the plane, took a deep breath and instantly, with no effort whatsoever, became Australian. It was like a switch flipped and he was an Aussie.

Thankfully, my new boss who had offered me the job in Singapore was there to greet us with a smile that stretched from ear to ear. He drove us to our rented accommodation in North Adelaide, a leafy inner-city suburb that looked like it had stepped right out of a Home and Garden magazine. He'd even brought along a child booster seat for the car and a bicycle for Amy, who was looking at this new chapter with the kind of enthusiasm only a four-year-old could muster. My new colleagues whom I had yet to meet, had prepared a bag of animated DVDs for her – such kindness was enough to put a slight pause in my grumbling. As I sat in the front seat of the car gazing out at an alien landscape, I silently promised myself that I would curb my complaining and make the best of things.

To start, I began to create my own little piece of England in our rented home. First step was to upturn all the garden furniture. I had read that Australia was home to more poisonous critters than anywhere else on Earth – with creatures that wanted to kill you 'just because'. And while LNT relaxed with a cold stubbie of beer, I braced myself for the impending apocalypse of deadly spiders and snakes.

'Those toxic creatures are only in the Hollywood movies,' LNT chuckled, watching me in bemusement, no doubt picturing himself with RM Williams gear, an Akubra hat and a slow drawl forming as he embraced his new Aussie persona.

'Just the movies, eh?' I snarled back, as the first upturned chair revealed a massive red-back spider scurrying to the safety of a crack in the paving. 'That's an eight-legged pearly gater right fucking there, and this is no movie, it's our new home in hot and dangerous Australia,' I moaned, my voice tinged with disbelief.

I could almost hear the poor landlord's thoughts as he received the first of many calls from his new tenants who he'd been assured were a delightful English couple. 'Hi, we're your new tenants, just flown in from the UK and we've found the house teeming with poisonous animals,' I said matter-of-factly. 'Fancy coming over to exorcise the place?'

It wasn't just Australia's terrifying fauna that knocked me sideways. Nothing could prepare me for my first visit to the local supermarket. Everything felt overwhelming and way more expensive than I had anticipated, and the labyrinth of foreign brands left me feeling homesick. That is until the glimmer of purple familiarity appeared. I leaped forward and hugged the bottle of Britain's finest purple creation – Ribena. It was a little slice of home in the form of sugary syrup, and I clung to it like a lifeline, despite the bonkers twelve-dollar price tag. The weird names of the bread brands and varieties of washing powder didn't help either, nor did the currency that refused to make sense. My brain was in full overload mode.

By New Year's Eve, I was ready to share my dissatisfaction with LNT, who by now had fully embraced Aussie life – flip-flops (thongs), vest (singlet), and a growing repertoire of 'g'day, maaate' and 'no worries'.

'I hate it here. We've made a huge mistake!' I vented.

Ever my rock, LNT remained unshaken, offering me the perspective I sorely needed. 'It's early days, Love. No one said it would be easy. But you have to remind yourself why we're here,' he said with calm certainty. 'The sun. Every morning it's right there, smiling down on us. The clothes dry in five minutes. The people speak the same language. They drive on the same side of the road, and there are beautiful, largely deserted beaches with crystal clear water, just waiting for us to explore.'

Suddenly I could see it. He was right. Clothes do dry in five minutes – maybe we were exactly where we needed to be. But that didn't stop me from casting a shadow on the positives. 'The washing might well dry in five minutes, but it ends up a very different colour after the sun has bleached it to a crisp,' I declared. 'And don't be surprised the beaches are deserted... they're probably teeming with crocodiles hiding in the dunes, ready to eat Poms. And what's the good of a crystal clear sea when it's home to a sixteen-mile-long jellyfish that paralyses you with its sting, leaving you to drown while – thanks to the clear water – you watch your feet turn blue! Not to mention the giant man-eating sharks everywhere. Fuck me, you've gone all Stockholm you have!'

LNT just chuckled and took another sip of his beer, knowing full well that despite my complaints, I really did enjoy getting the bed linen dry in five minutes.

I struggled to deal with the grief that came from the loss of familiarity. I grappled unsuccessfully with the loneliness and the vulnerability that migration invoked, crying myself to sleep most nights for the first year. I had thought I was worldly and up for anything, but it turned out, the pull of where I called home was far stronger than I'd anticipated, and for this I had absolutely no coping strategy.

23

Out Back

When you find yourself stranded on the other side of the world, grappling with everything from a new job running a regional prison, to a Knight Rider car called Kitt, it's easy to feel lost. The disconnect between what you thought life would be like and the reality of living in a foreign land can be overwhelming. But what if the very thing that feels like an unbearable challenge is in fact, the key to discovering the best version of yourself?

An English woman who had migrated to Australia a few years earlier helped put my struggles into perspective at a social gathering we attended shortly after our arrival.

'You need to be kind to yourself,' she said after I had latched onto her and poured out my tormented soul. 'It's going to take at least two years to really feel comfortable in your new surroundings, so don't fight it,' she added, her voice as soothing as a cup of Yorkshire tea. She gave me – the whiny resident of Whine Street – a comforting hug. 'It will take time. You can't rush it. Just trust that it will pass and one day you'll love it here. Believe me, I've been through all the desolation you're feeling right now and emerged a happy expatriate.'

I could hardly believe that someone from my homeland could suggest such turncoat emotions! She had clearly been brainwashed or possibly exposed to too much harsh sunlight, in addition to going all Stockholm on me too. Yet, on another level, her words resonated with me and provided a compass to keep me moving forward. However, I just couldn't find the stamina to be optimistic and my days of sulking like a teenager continued. Still, I clung to the reassurance that if it all went wrong, if the horizon didn't hold happiness, LNT had agreed that after two years, we'd pack up and go home – leaving the sunshine behind us.

On January 16th, 2012, I stepped out from my deadly-spider infested rental property in North Adelaide, hopped into my keyless car and drove the four kilometres into the city for my first day at work. I'd never owned or driven one of these keyless wonders before, so it was a novelty to press a button to start the car. It gave me a little lift, knowing that amidst all the pain and gloom, there were still signs I was living in a very privileged world.

Day One was a blur of meetings with my new boss. We pored over the finer details of my role as the General Manager of a flagship regional prison some sixty kilometres from the city. I was introduced to the other senior executives and I got the impression I was in the temporary calmness at the centre of a tornado.

'That's it for today,' my boss finally said, just after five o'clock. 'Have a great first day tomorrow. I'll walk you to your car,' he added with a warm smile.

The smile transformed into hearty laughter at the expense of this 'Pommy Sheila' when we arrived at my car. My boss looked at it quizzically, placed his palm on the bonnet and declared that it felt unusually hot.

'Well, the sun's been shining, and my car's been in its glare for about eight hours,' I said a little smart-arsedly.

'No, I think you have left the engine running,' he suggested, eyes twinkling with mischief.

Oh my God, I thought. Here I am trying to make a star-studded start to a new career and showcase my vast intellect, and I've left my fucking car running *all* day. I was mortified. 'I thought it would be clever enough to switch itself off when I hopped out,' I stammered, utterly defeated.

Day Two at the prison had to be better. After all, I was an unknown, and that was an enormous advantage. I could be whoever I wanted to be. I could reinvent myself. It was an intoxicating thought, but right then I didn't have the strength for a full-on makeover. Besides, I was comfortable with who I was. So, I walked in as me – the newly arrived Pom General Manager – aka 'Gov'.

As I surveyed the room, I noticed one of the prison officers deeply engrossed in the morning newspaper. An agitated twitch took hold of me, followed by a rapid rise in my temperature at the sheer audacity of this guy openly turning the pages while I was speaking. In that moment, I imagined myself marching over and telling him to take a long hike off a short pier, but then I remembered – *I* was the boss. As annoying as it was, I had to keep my mouth shut for now.

As I navigated through the prison, familiarising myself with its people and facilities, I soon came to realise that it was a world away from the big, thick-walled Victorian versions of prisons I was familiar with.

Absenteeism was a fair bit higher than what I'd seen back in the UK – perhaps unsurprising with all the human-jerky-making UV from the sun, shark, spider and snake bites and possibly a roll with a crocodile...

I'd naively assumed that because we spoke the same language, the work culture would be the same. Wrong. If I was going to make it in this new role, I had a lot to learn – and fast. I spent my first few weeks walking around the prison with my eyebrows a solid six inches higher than usual – a sign that it was time for Botox.

But despite all the quirks, the prison had a certain homeliness about it. The people were warm and welcoming, and I quickly spotted opportunities to build on the work done by those before me. Of course, it wasn't all smooth sailing...

Thankfully, the prisoners were, for the most part, well-behaved, and far more compliant and agreeable than their UK counterparts. After all, Aussies are a more laid-back bunch. My new prison also had a very different crime demographic compared to what I was used to. There were no Eastern European crime syndicates or the diverse array of London's troubled gangs and criminal circles.

My first few months were spent getting across the many unfamiliar prison policies, and trying to get to know my staff. It wasn't always easy, but with each passing day, I could feel myself feeling more at ease.

One afternoon, as we wandered around the vast red sand perimeter of the prison, I turned to my new executive assistant and asked, 'Is this the outback?'

She laughed. 'No, Boss, we're barely out of the city. The outback is a few hundred kilometres that way.' She pointed north.

As you might expect, building relationships and driving change in an unfamiliar environment came with its fair share of challenges, including the occasional run-in with the trade unions.

I can honestly say that none of my battles were personal. Every decision I made was rooted in the best interests of the service. But I won't lie – it was emotionally and physically exhausting. Being the first female General Manager at the prison added some spice to the mix. Throw in the fact that I was an opinionated Pom, and it's easy to imagine how that might polarise people's views about my appointment.

Then there was Bob. Bob was a big, burly country man, macho as hell, and beloved by everyone. He'd been around for years, loyal to the cause, and always the life of the party. He was the epitome of the perfect Aussie prison officer and a trusted leader in the incident response team, responsible for handling riotous prisoners. I've always been a firm believer in using the minimum force necessary to control and contain a situation. Years of experience had taught me that unless you're dealing with someone with serious mental health issues, your voice is your greatest ally. When big, burly, and bronzed Bob sauntered into my office to inform me that a nearby prison was struggling to get an uncooperative prisoner to leave their cell for a court appearance, he asked me to sign off on a mechanical restraint request, complete with pepper spray. I refused. I wasn't about to start my legacy by endorsing maximum force when I believed the situation could be handled with a little more finesse. I suggested he try using his interpersonal skills instead.

It's safe to say that what I had communicated didn't come across as I'd hoped. He insisted that he knew the prisoner far better than I did and was certain of how things would unfold. Before I could respond, he turned on his heels and abruptly left my office.

Five hours later, Bob strolled back in, looking irritated to be in my presence. He matter-of-factly announced that he had managed to talk the prisoner out of the cell without using force. Just as I was about to congratulate him, he added that although he would never have used mechanical restraints as a first option, he had to have them authorised 'just in case'. He then tossed the paperwork onto my desk and walked out without another word.

That night, I shared the encounter with LNT. 'It's so different here. Maybe it's me,' I said, self-doubt creeping into my voice. 'I assumed because we speak the same language, the culture would be the same. But it's just... so different. I'm not sure I'm going to make it here.'

The next morning a soft knock at my office door pulled me from my mountain of paperwork. I looked up to find Bob standing in my doorway, his posture less rigid than before. He walked toward me slowly, extended his hand, and said, 'My name is Bob. Nice to meet you. Can we start again?'

With genuine sincerity, I took his massive man-hand. 'Yes, we can, Bob,' I said. 'I'm pleased to meet you too.'

This was the day I made a shift in how I was showing up, moving from 'I' to 'We', and I felt a surge of belonging rush through my veins at last.

I went on to make Bob one of my senior leaders. Looking back, I realised he was frustrated by my lack of curiosity and translated my message as an unfair judgement of his professionalism. My tired, defensive response had only made matters worse. Once we cleared the air, I saw the brilliance in him that had always been there. Through all the challenges we faced, Bob remained a steadfast and exemplary lieutenant, and an all-round good egg.

Those first few hectic weeks were the baptism of fire I needed. The monumental task of learning a new world and running a prison with an unfamiliar culture took my mind off any lingering self-absorption. My new work family were fucking awesome – I just needed to open my eyes to celebrate their difference.

24

Cuntessa

Name-calling can cut deep, but in the world of prisons the adage: 'sticks and stones may break my bones, but words will never hurt me' rings truer than ever. In prison, the best way to handle a cruel nickname is to transform it into a badge of honour. Wit becomes a shield – diffusing hostility, building camaraderie, and ultimately helping to create a sense of belonging.

Much like the scorching, arid surroundings of my new workplace were a far cry from the lush countryside of my birthplace, I felt like an anomaly amidst the red dust of regional South Australia. But armed with a no-nonsense attitude, I was ready to tackle the many hurdles of prison management. Though I had been hired for exactly that purpose, my lack of history in this new land made me feel on the back foot and vulnerable. I was making changes, and those changes ruffled the feathers of a couple of... let's refer to them as the 'silly ones'. Their disdain for me was palpable.

It wasn't long before one of my senior leaders approached me with the news that I had acquired a colourful nickname. He reassured me that Aussies were notorious for handing out nicknames and that I should take it as a compliment. I listened to his spiel, all while recalling the few kind and the many less-than-flattering nicknames I'd collected over the years.

'Okay, I have had a few in my time,' I said, goading him. 'I was once "Barbie" – apparently, I was a ditzy blonde back in the day. Then there was the no-explanation-needed "Bumfront". So, what have you lot come up with?'

He hesitated, then sheepishly replied, 'I'm not sure I should be the one to tell you, Boss.'

It was one of those moments when pressing the issue might not be the best idea. Still, I shrugged it off, trying to play it down. 'Hey, having a nickname might be cool,' I said, before hitting him with my infamous you-had-better-tell-me-or-I-will-torture-you look. He stood there in silence, locked in a stare-down, while I waited patiently for him to crack.

'*Cuntessa...*' he finally muttered, surrendering in the standoff.

I kept a stern, professional expression, fighting the urge to burst into raucous laughter at the sheer ingenuity of it. It was undoubtedly the most fitting nickname I'd ever had. It definitely ranked high on the scale of inappropriateness, and it was so unapologetically Australian.

That evening, I recounted the day's events, sharing the nickname episode with LNT.

'I admit it's pretty funny,' I said with a grin, 'even if it is a world away from the prison environment I'm used to.'

LNT could be a bit prissy at times, especially when the 'c' word was thrown around, but even he couldn't help but crack up. Once his laughter subsided and he had regained his composure, he added, 'It's one of the most fitting nicknames for you I've ever heard.'

I raised an eyebrow, my tone mildly hurt. 'Fitting? What exactly do you mean by that?'

LNT, ever the diplomat, quickly found his footing. He explained that by 'fitting', he meant it captured the persona of a female General Manager like me.

'After all, you've made a couple of people quite rightfully uncomfortable,' he reassured me. 'You've also tackled some big issues like drug smuggling.' Somehow LNT managed to convince me that despite its crudeness, the nickname was indeed a back-handed compliment.

That night, I tossed and turned in bed, my mind wrestling with how to respond to the whole 'Cuntessa' episode. I realised I had three options. The first was to fight fire with fire, but I quickly dismissed that as a kneejerk reaction. It carried the risk of turning a small spark into a full-blown inferno. After all, I reminded myself, there's wisdom in the saying that a moment of patience in a moment of anger can save a thousand moments of regret.

Second, I could ignore it, remain poker faced, and I could carry on as if it didn't happen. Or the third option was that I could compromise. I could ensure that the prison did its job fairly and humanely – making sure no prisoner died or escaped on my watch – but, at the same time, send a clear message to anyone who was uncomfortable having a strong woman at the helm.

I decided the third option would make it known that I was committed to increasing the number of women on my leadership teams. That would be the takeaway, and for it to truly resonate, the delivery had to be creative.

The idea hit me that weekend when I was flicking through the glossy pages of an interior design magazine while waiting in line at the supermarket check-out. The properties in the magazine were stunning, each one showcasing an unmistakable feminine touch.

'That's it!' I blurted out loud, earning a few puzzled looks from the people ahead of me in the queue.

Based on my experience, the best way to support a new culture was to ensure the environment reflected it. And, of course, I could add a generous sprinkle of the feminine touch.

'What better way to respond to a Cuntessa nickname than by building myself a castle?' I chuckled as I packed my groceries into the car and drove home, my mind racing with excitement at the possibilities.

While a real castle was out of reach, I could transform my office into a palace. But not just any palace – a vaginal pink palace, with corridors leading to what I would dub 'Cuntessa's Citadel', painted in a striking shade of purple. This wouldn't just freak out the silly ones who were easily offended, but it would also reinforce the prison's diversity and equality stance, which had chosen purple as its campaign colour. After all, purple is a blend of the wisdom of blue and the passion of red – symbols of justice.

The following Monday brought with it one clear priority, which was to speak with the person I had identified to be my tradie for the week. Jacko was an elderly inmate serving life for murder, and he was a gifted painter. Despite his dark past, he had transformed into an institutionalised prisoner, and I saw in him someone whose skills could be harnessed for something meaningful.

'Jacko,' I said, as he stood awkwardly in my doorway. 'How would you feel if I asked you to help me with a little project?'

'No worries, ma'am,' he replied, not even bothering to ask what it would entail.

He found it quite amusing when I told him he would be painting my office pink, with the corridors leading to it a bold, distinctive purple. Jacko saw it as an honour to be chosen for the task. Regardless of his past, Jacko was always eager to apply his talents. It was satisfying to watch him work; his enthusiasm for the project was infectious. Each day he arrived with a smile, courteous and diligent, occasionally stepping back to admire his progress. When he did, his gaze would shift to me, awaiting an affirmative nod. And, sometimes, there was a cheeky smirk, as if he knew exactly why I was doing it.

With my pink palace now complete, I decided to host the grand opening of Cuntessa's Citadel. The bold décor, with its vibrant pink hues and purple corridors, certainly caused a stir. The silly ones who seemed to take offence at my very existence were especially vocal, questioning my sanity.

One of them took it a step further, making a point to express his disapproval each time we had a meeting. His protest? Flatly refusing to sit in the chair I offered him, choosing instead to stand with his arms folded.

'Aaaw, c'mon, mate,' I would say. 'Take a seat.'

'I'm good, I'm just fine standing,' came his inevitable, crusty reply.

He stood rigidly throughout each meeting like a soldier at attention. My strategy? To drag out the meetings as long as possible, just to make him squirm a little more. Deep down, I hoped that the longer he stood in the pink surroundings, the more likely he'd loosen up – or at least begin to see me as friend and not foe. Unfortunately, he proved irredeemable. Instead of evolving, he launched into a sexist joke one day, standing there like an immovable monument.

'Boss,' he said with a smug grin creeping across his face, 'how do you know when a woman is about to say something smart?'

I gave him a look of disinterest, barely concealing my cyclone-force sigh.

'When she starts her sentence with, "A man once told me..."' he chortled.

While he remained firmly entrenched in his antiquated views, many of my new colleagues had a very different reaction to the Pink Palace – and they absolutely loved it. Some even went above and beyond, adding their own touches of homeliness and femininity. One day, they gifted me what I initially thought was just a regular Australian native plant. With zero horticultural knowledge, I saw it only as a 'thingamabob' plant. But they assured me that although it appeared to be a modest, green-leafed nonentity, with care and attention, it would eventually sprout a spectacularly tall pink flower. They were right... though unfortunately, I wasn't there to witness its inaugural bloom.

LNT, ever the advocate for balance, suggested we take a family holiday. Reluctantly, I agreed and soon found myself preparing to hand over the reins to a capable short-term replacement. Along with my handover, I created a detailed 'to do' list, at the very top of which, in big bold letters, was the First Commandment: *Take good care of my plant!*

Two weeks later, after soaking up the Californian sunshine, I returned to find that my stand-in had done an excellent job. No one had died or escaped, no buildings had fallen, and thankfully, my plant had flourished.

It stood tall and lush, now boasting a resplendent pink flower, even more beautiful than I had imagined.

'How could this be?' I asked my executive assistant, feeling slightly betrayed. 'Surely my plant wouldn't choose to flower for the first time while I was away?'

'Maybe it prefers your poxy proxy,' she replied with a knowing smirk.

A few days later, she sidled up to me. 'I need to tell you something about while you were away...' she whispered, clearly hiding a secret.

Intrigued, I sank into my chair and motioned for her to spill the beans.

'Your plant wasn't a two-timing cheat,' she said, speaking slowly and deliberately. 'After you'd been gone for about a week, a pungent whiff emanated from your office. Your stand-in didn't seem bothered, so I tried to ignore it. However, when the stench reached unbearable levels, that's when I was forced to investigate. While your stand-in was in a meeting, I tiptoed around the office to find the source of the smell. I was relieved it wasn't your poxy proxy, but unfortunately, it was your plant. He'd overwatered it and it had drowned, leaving it limp and rotting. We dashed out to buy a replacement so you wouldn't know, but the only one we could find was flowering!'

The surrogate plant quickly became the new jewel in my little work oasis.

Cuntessa had survived her first round of prison life Down Under.

Rising above cruel labels, and using humour to turn challenges into growth opportunities, helped me find my place in the world. Ultimately, it's not the world that defines us, it's how we choose to engage with it.

25

She's Well Hard!

In a place where logic had packed its bags, left the building, and moved back to a beach in Majorca, unpredictability was crowned king. I quickly learned that the only way to survive was to face each absurdity head-on while clinging on for dear life to my values. Between reading a colleague their last rites one minute and locking eyes with the world's second most venomous snake the next, I was treated to moments of pure comedy that taught me more about humanity than any self-help book could.

The first year in an Australian prison? Tough. It felt like I'd signed up for a workplace training course... on steroids. But I was more determined than I'd ever been. There were some things I simply wouldn't budge on, no matter how much smoother it would have made my life. Tackling those things became an all-consuming mission, one that made everything else seem like a footnote.

Failure wasn't an option. If I was to succeed, I had to get up close and personal with every square centimetre of my prison – from the buildings to the sprawling grounds, and everyone inhabiting it. So I dived in headfirst, sleeves rolled up, ready for action. Once I had a handle on the administrative and prison buildings, it was time to scope out the perimeter. Enter Kenny – larger than life, perpetually chewing a toothpick, and sporting a kind of dry humour you only get from spending too much time under the blistering Aussie sun. On a particularly scorching summer's day, I managed to talk him into joining me for an expedition to the wilderness at the edge of the prison grounds.

As we trudged towards the boundary fence, something glimmered in the distance.

'What's that?' I asked, squinting at the shimmer.

'That's an old disused greenhouse, Boss,' Kenny said, as chilled as ever. Naturally, my curiosity got the better of me and I suggested we hike up the hill for a closer look.

As we neared the rundown structure, a sense of unease crept over me. Please don't let there be a huge cannabis crop in there, I silently prayed. Thankfully, the greenhouse was empty, but what caught my eye was a large tank propped up against one of its decaying aluminium-framed glass walls.

'And what is that?' I asked, pointing.

'That's a worm farm, Boss,' Kenny replied, his tone as casual as if I'd asked about the weather.

'A worm farm?' I raised my eyebrow or at least tried to – by this point I'd surrendered to the temptations of Botox.

'Yep, a worm farm,' he repeated, his heat-induced drawl thickening.

'I know I'm English, but don't take the piss. Who the hell farms worms?' I quizzed.

Kenny twirled his toothpick as he assured me he wasn't pulling my leg. He bent down, turned on a tap at the base of the tank, and released a dark, gooey liquid.

'You see that? That's the product of the worm farm. It's used to fertilise plants,' he explained. He then grabbed an old terracotta pot from the ground, lifted the lid off the tank, and scooped out some of the contents, revealing a wriggling army of worms.

'See, Boss? I shit you not, it's a worm farm!' Kenny said, clearly thrilled about being proved right.

As I marvelled at Kenny's triumphant moment and the mind-blowing revelation that I was not well-versed in the finer points of worm farming

– I noticed something else. The back of Kenny's pale blue prison shirt was absolutely swarming with bees. Apparently, the little guys had been happily living under the lid of the worm farm until Kenny's enthusiastic digging stirred up their wrath.

'Fuck, Kenny, fuck, fuck!' I yelled, at which point Kenny's triumphant grin morphed into sheer panic. We both looked up just in time to witness a thick, angry cloud of bees – so black and dense it could've passed for a freaky solar eclipse. For a moment, it did block out the sunlight, which would've been cool to catch on camera if I wasn't too busy imagining the bees' evil plans to kill us both.

'Ruuuuuuunnnnn!' I bellowed, pointing downhill towards the distant speck of a makeshift storage facility about one kilometre away.

Kenny didn't need any encouragement. He shot off like a greyhound, but his gallop quickly turned into an out-of-control disaster. There was a blur of flailing limbs and raw momentum that had him tumbling down the hill like a boulder on roller skates. At one point, his foot caught on a rock, sending him into an impromptu pirouette that would've impressed any ballet instructor if it hadn't been doomed from the start.

I swear I saw his life flash before his eyes as he spun towards the ground like an out-of-control stuntman. With a catastrophic crash mere milliseconds away, I finally caught up to him, just in time for him to let out a blood-curdling scream. His outstretched hands slapped my back, a bizarre mix of desperation to break his fall and equally desperate attempts to ward off the angry swarm now zooming towards us like a squadron of fighter jets.

In a panic, I began flailing at his upper back, trying to shoo away the swarm. But it was too late – Kenny's face was now the prime target, and the bees seemed intent on turning him a shade of red that not even the Australian sun could match. His cheeks turned crimson, and the bees seemed to multiply as if auditioning for a role in *The Swarm*.

I swung at his face, trying to give him some temporary relief, but every time I landed a strike, he'd scream louder and hit me right back, his hand connecting with my jaw resulting in what could only be described as a desperate, bee-induced slap fight.

'This is how it's going to end, Kenny!' I yelled over the chaos, dodging one of his wildly flailing limbs. 'We're gonna die in some naff *Keystone Cops* routine, but at least our grandkids will have an epic story to tell: "... and that's how Nan and Grandad died – succumbed to a swarming death of vengeance and stingy justice!"'

Breathless and covered in swarming bees, we both looked ahead, only to spot a white van doing a boundary fence check. The security guard behind the wheel looked utterly bewildered as she slammed on the brakes, her mouth hanging open in pure, confused shock. Even with limited lip-reading skills I could make out what she was saying. 'What the fuuuuuuuck...' she mouthed, clearly unable to process the chaotic scene unfolding before her eyes.

She grabbed the communication radio, clearly assuming she was witnessing a full-blown showdown between the new General Manager and a much-loved colleague. In a panic, she sent out the standard 'emergency' message, as if we were in the middle of a prison-wide crisis situation. The response was instant. All the security cameras suddenly whirred to life, swivelling and zooming in on us as if we were the stars of a really messed up reality show.

Word spread faster than a viral TikTok. The rumour mill went into overdrive, and within minutes, the entire prison was convinced that Cuntessa had just entered a full-blown brawl with poor, gentle Kenny. Naturally, with Cuntessa in the ring, it wasn't just a fight – it was confirmation that she wasn't just a regular, garden-variety cunt, but a violent, bee-chasing, chaos-stirring, menace-to-society cunt.

Kenny and I, sensing imminent death and desperate for refuge from both the bees and each other, spotted a small outpost building that could serve as our safe house. We made a mad 'beeline' for it, charging down the hill in a frantic dash with a squillion bees as our entourage. We crashed through the front door like a couple of football players bursting through a pre-match banner, scaring the absolute bejesus out of the poor guy inside. He was only about a month away from his well-earned retirement, likely daydreaming about pottering about in his garden – until two bee-infested lunatics stormed in.

'I'm allergic to bees!' he yelped, his face draining of colour as he dived under his desk, presumably hoping that some under-desk magic shield would save him from the wrath of nature's tiny but vicious warriors.

A mirror on the wall revealed my battle scars. One eyelid had swollen so much my eye was almost completely closed and I looked like I'd just taken a beating from Mike Tyson.

Poor Kenny had collapsed to the floor, utterly exhausted and, I can only assume, with about a hundred bee stings plastered across his face. I could only imagine what the people watching via the security cameras were saying, 'Did you see that? Cuntessa threw a punch, and Kenny went down like a ragdoll!'

Panicked, I called for an ambulance, convinced that Kenny had gone into anaphylactic shock and was about to exit this world with a dramatic flatline. In that moment, I couldn't help but mentally recite his last rites, imagining his obituary as a headline, *Beloved Kenny, gone too soon – victim of bees and Cuntessa's poor decision-making.*

The medics arrived and scrambled to stabilise him. Kenny, ever the trooper, managed a weak thumbs-up as they carted him away on a stretcher – the trusty toothpick somehow still protruding from his mouth.

I returned to my office, my face still throbbing and looking like I'd just gone twelve rounds. But Cuntessa hadn't lost the battle just yet! I sprang into action, arranging for the bees to be smoked out of their sanctuary. By the time the sun set on that absurdly eventful day, the tiny terrorists had shuffled off their mortal coils, and I could finally take a breath without fearing an ambush when I left the administration building.

After a brief hospital stay, I was relieved to hear that Kenny had been declared out of danger. After a course of treatment and a few days' rest, he was back to his old self – albeit with a bit of a bee phobia.

The following morning at the all-staff muster, there was a faint hum from the back of the room – an innocuous drone that seemed harmless enough. But with each name called during roll call, it grew louder, more insistent, until it was unmistakably like bees buzzing. At first, I tried to hold back my laughter, but then I let out a chuckle, and before I knew it the whole room erupted into laughter with me. Yep, the bee legacy was very much alive – still buzzing and stinging in the form of a hilarious chorus that serenaded me for the next few days at muster. And with that, I realised I had not only survived a kamikaze bee attack, but I had officially been inducted as their General Manager, and the pain of every one of those stings had been so bloody worth it.

Kenny and I were reunited for weekly campus tours, though we wisely upgraded from walking to cruising around in a golf buggy. We had learnt a valuable lesson – meddling in far off deserted buildings could get us killed. I chalked it up as another notch in my ongoing education of dangerous things in Australia – and its rather unique 'outback' prison.

Kenny's knowledge was sometimes a bit... questionable, but he delivered it with such humour, that it was hard not to enjoy the ride. During one of our tours, I pointed to some large, green spikey balls scattered around the grounds and waited for Kenny to come up with some outlandish backstory. 'What are those?' I asked, looking at him like he was my personal Aussie Wikipedia.

'Paddy melons, Boss,' he replied. 'You can eat 'em but they give you the shits and you'll go blind.'

I became utterly fascinated by the kangaroos that roamed the grounds flanking the prison. These creatures were not only everywhere, but they also had one peculiar obsession – getting into the prison. So, while we spent our days trying to stop prisoners breaking out, these goofy marsupials spent their days trying to break in. They'd stand at the fence, sizing it up, then in a moment of wild inspiration, they'd charge at it. Their powerful hind legs would engage, and they'd leap into the air with all the elegance of an Olympic pole-vaulter, only to crash, mid-fence, and tumble back down to earth in a confused heap. Looking utterly perplexed, they'd get up, dust themselves off, puff out their chests, and try it again. The more experienced kangaroos would even take a few steps back, as if planning a more effective approach. Spoiler alert: It didn't work. But that didn't stop these deluded creatures from giving it their all. Every. Single. Time.

Each time I witnessed one of these absurd, yet endearing, kangaroo attempts, I couldn't help thinking of the expression Aussie's use to infer someone's crazy: *They've got a kangaroo loose in the top paddock.*

But I wonder how humans would fare if we had even half the determination of Australia's national animal. If we did, maybe we'd be more comfortable with failure and always ready to give it another go.

Snakes were one of the many sources of both fascination and fear for us Brits. But fascination for me won out, so I asked one of the prisoners who worked in the gardens to show me a snake if ever he came across one.

'Nurries, Boss,' he assured me, using the Aussie shorthand for 'no worries'.

True to his word, a few days later, I was sitting in my office when I heard a tap on my pink office window. I turned to find the smiling gardener holding a long brown angrily writhing creature just below its neck.

'Here's your snake, Boss,' he said cheerfully. 'It's a brown snake, one of the most venomous in the world, responsible for about sixty per cent of all snake bite deaths in Straya.' He paused, looking at me with an almost childlike sincerity. 'Shall I bring it in so you can have a proper look, Boss?'

Now, as much as a snake in my Pink Palace had a certain Cleopatra-like appeal, I politely declined and suggested he take it somewhere it could 'visit the angels'.

'It's illegal to kill 'em, Boss. Besides, they've got a job to do here. I'll take it back to where I found it.'

My Botoxed eyebrows shot up as high as they could go. Here was a man serving life for murder, casually explaining to me the legalities and ethics of killing a snake. I rolled my eyes, fully aware that life behind bars was anything but ordinary – no matter where in the world you were.

My education didn't end with the local wildlife. Some of the humans I encountered were equally eye-opening. One day, a member of my team, who quickly and secretly became one of my favourite humans of all time, kindly offered to take me to lunch in town. Intrigued, I agreed and soon found myself in his Ute. It was my first time in one, and I couldn't help but notice it had a carpeted dashboard. What on earth was that for?

As he popped on his hat with corks hanging from the brim and walked around to the driver's side, I muttered, 'Who is this guy?' Thoughts of true crime in the outback suddenly flooded my mind from the many Australian murder documentaries I'd seen. As we bounced out of the pot-holed prison car park, I found myself wondering, am I about to be murdered? Stuffed into a barrel? Locked in some dark vault?

As wild as my latest prison adventure was, I look back on it with deep fondness. I needed that experience, and I grew to love it – along with the incredible staff I met along the way – even the 'silly ones'.

Sometimes, we have to wade through the uncomfortable stuff to learn something truly valuable – whether it's about snakes, people, or ourselves. My time in South Australian prisons taught me an important lesson: just because I think I'm right, doesn't mean the other person is wrong.

26

I'm In...

What do you do when you've spent years hopping between careers that make no logical sense to the reader of your CV? Well... you create the perfect storm – armed with desperation, humour, and just the right amount of recklessness. Then you let those unexpected moments push you forward – even when you're completely lost.

I had joined the prison service purely because it offered a few pounds more than the flight attendant gig alongside it in that life-changing issue of *The Daily Telegraph*. Surprisingly, what followed was a career in which I thrived. I loved working with the officers and the inmates, but the higher up I moved, the more I was bogged down in a bureaucratic mess of endless emails and meetings, and risked losing touch with the frontline.

Ultimately, my decision to leave the prison service stemmed from an unrelenting desire not to grow old in one career. Even though prison work had become one of the few growth industries during the global financial crisis, it no longer excited me.

I was occasionally asked to serve as an executive in head office, which did help to keep me energised, but it wasn't enough – my ego had got itchy feet again!

I didn't fancy moving interstate to run a huge prison again, or want to go back to the UK, as I had come to love South Australia – its charm, its pace, and its people.

I had loved the commercial aspect of my role as a Controller back in the UK, which had ignited a hunger to develop my business acumen. It was time to spread my wings and take flight, even if the future was unclear for someone neither born nor schooled in a city that placed great weight to both.

My CEO was incredibly supportive when I told him of my decision to leave. He said something that put a little spring back in my step. 'You've been an asset to the South Australian prison system and have made such an impact that I'm sure your future will be bright, no matter what path you choose.' He went on to insist on hosting a farewell dinner in my honour.

I was floored by the presence of some of the most influential people in the State's criminal justice system. As I welcomed them to the feast, I couldn't help but feel a little overwhelmed. The conversation was flowing well when my CEO, one of those who had interviewed me at that riverside restaurant in Singapore, decided to take the conversation in a different direction. He looked over at me and tapped his glass to grab everyone's attention.

'Well, now that you have come full circle, why don't you tell everyone how it all started, back in Singapore?' he said with a mischievous grin spreading across his face.

'What exactly are you getting at?' I asked, a little confused.

'You know, the squid episode,' he chuckled. 'We saw how much you hated that squid, how you battled to pretend it was delicious as you forced every scratchy, disgusting mouthful down your throat. We've dined out on that story and laughed about it for years.' The room fell silent, all eyes turning to me.

I gave them the performance of a lifetime, reliving the squid nightmare with full theatrics. 'That's how much I wanted the fucking job!' I concluded.

'We saw that,' my boss shot back. 'That's what got you the job – your sheer bloody-mindedness!'

It was a perfect moment of camaraderie and the ideal way to close the prison chapter.

The determination to reinvent myself was all-consuming and I wasn't one to take things slowly. I craved pace, and the thought of a slow transition from government to the private sector didn't sit well with me. The next day I woke up, and without checking my parachute, jumped straight out of the plane, hoping for the best. I applied for all the locally-based executive jobs I saw advertised.

Weeks turned into months, and the responses boomeranged back with the same 'we regret to inform you' message. The harsh realisation hit me – despite being pretty good at leading large-scale operations, I was an unknown outside the criminal justice world. I had no network, no established foothold, and was effectively starting from scratch.

It was time to dust off the successes of 1996 and do some serious thinking. I pimped myself out, not in the madam sense, of course, but by returning to the healthier side of the Club 18-30 *modus operandi* – networking. I networked aggressively as if my next meal depended on it. I talked to strangers, sent out LinkedIn and Facebook invitations, and asked everyone I met if they could introduce me to another business connection.

The only way to describe how I felt was how I imagined a puppy in a pet shop must feel. Day after day people walk in, stop for a moment, glance at the puppy and say, 'Oh, you're adorable... but you can't come home with me as there isn't any room.' Every day ends with the puppy feeling rejected.

A backlog of job applications piled up, and I had only two interviews to show for it – both of which I didn't win. Then came my first break. A friend of a friend who was aware of my plight, offered me a three-week contracting assignment re-writing policies for a Guide Dogs Organisation. At this point, I had practically given up on the thought of ever being an executive again.

As a lifelong cat person with little connection to dogs, this position tested my resolve. And just three days into the job, it morphed into me being asked to head up the organisation's operations. This was more in line with my leadership experience, and I thought maybe I hadn't given dogs a fair go. Maybe we'd grow to love each other.

Dogs were in my office every day, tethered to my desk while waiting for their training sessions in the yard. One day, while deep in discussion with the CEO, one of these hounds decided to curl one off right in front of me – about a foot away and on my office carpet, touching the side of my long raincoat hanging over my chair. I didn't know whether to laugh or cry and I was scared to move in case the vibration would make this steaming castle tumble onto my new beige Burberry mac.

'How has my professional life come to this? I've swapped human shit for dog shit!' I nervously laughed. 'I'm working in a tiny cubicle with a fucking dog I don't like, who's rubbing white dog hair all over my black work trousers, then stands up and without warning shits a soft serve right in front of me. And, worse still, it's my job to clean it up!'

Laughter was by far my favourite medicine, and it was never far away in this role. My responsibilities were varied and included managing the breeding program and overseeing the veterinary staff. There was this one stud dog who always entered the building with the broadest dog smile you've ever seen. He knew exactly why he was there, and the excitement was palpable as Travis, our artificial inseminator vet, reached for the latex gloves to prepare for his role as the hound's gloved wife. The dog loved the glove, though it was unsettling to be around for the regular ritual. The dog would bounce into the room with a happy wagging tail, let out little shrieks of joy, and add a few joyful barks to the mix. Apparently, the dog-tug method was more effective than the traditional humping approach for producing puppies.

Though it was a tad unusual, my eighteen months at Guide Dogs was the perfect segue from government work to the private sector. The organisation had a huge heart that beat loud and strong, and it was good for my soul.

During my time there, the fateful opportunity to present at an international real estate seminar arose. 'I've never been a public speaker,' I confessed to my boss when the invitation came in, perhaps looking for an excuse to gracefully bow out. But she was having none of it, reassuring me that my storytelling ability would get me through. All I had to do was brush up on the topic of 'Resilience'.

I clearly misunderstood the brief. Just minutes into the presentation, I was confronted with stunned looks and jaws hitting the ground from the audience of mostly female executives, including a Chinese commercial property investor who was receiving my narrative through an interpreter. At that point, it was too late to change tack, and even if I could, I had nothing to fall back on. So I ploughed forward with all the gusto I could muster – sharing shit-story after shit-story.

'And that,' I said some twenty minutes later, 'brings my story to a close.'

A long eerie silence filled the room. I stared out at a sea of wide-eyed faces, silently praying for someone, anyone, to do something. Even a 'boo' or the odd flying object would've been a relief.

Then, at the back of the room, the Chinese investor stood up, clapping enthusiastically and bowing multiple times. The crowd, looking like they had just been handed an escape route, eagerly followed suit, rising to their feet in awkward unison. I had no idea what had just happened, but I was more than happy to take the standing ovation. As it turned out, the power of awkward humour and the universal appreciation for survival had made an impression after all.

The host CEO then stood up to deliver what sounded like the world's most backhanded compliment. 'I will struggle to come to terms with what I have just heard about your journey,' he said, his tone dripping with admiration – or it could have been pity? I couldn't quite tell if he was genuinely praising me or subtly implying my speech had been as welcome as a turd in the bathtub.

Surprisingly though, my presentation turned out to be the launchpad for the next phase in my professional life. The very next day, I received a text from someone claiming to be a CEO of a large financial institution, 'Hi, I've heard a lot about you. Can we meet for coffee?' Short, cryptic, and a bit mysterious. I had no idea who this person was or what he wanted, but I figured, what the hell...

That coffee meeting quickly snowballed into a tour of his company, followed by a promising introduction to his head of HR. Still, I wasn't entirely sure what role they thought I could fill. The conversation wrapped up with a surreal invitation to join him in a corporate box at a Taylor Swift concert that evening. Since LNT wasn't exactly a Swiftie, I took Amy along instead. The two of us danced to 'Shake it Off', while I tried to process just how bizarre this whole episode had turned out to be.

'So, have you given thought to my proposition?' my new CEO friend asked during the concert intermission.

Proposition? What proposition? I'd been so caught up in the lights, music and excitement that I'd completely forgotten what he was talking about. But I wasn't about to blow what could be the chance of a lifetime. With my heart pounding and adrenaline coursing through me, I gave the most professional response I could muster – shaking off the sweat from my brow, I fist-pumped and said, 'Yes, I have. I'm in...'

I mean, what professional fuckwit fist-pumps and says, 'I'm in?' And, 'in' for what? Was I volunteering for a heist? Joining a cult? At that exact moment, I couldn't have given a flying fuck. Whatever it was, I was in!

The mystery was solved the following Monday when I found myself sitting in his office discussing contract terms for a hefty executive role. The decision to take the position came down to pure ego – and, of course, the money. I remember thinking the Haverhill girl had done well for herself, and I was so proud of her.

It didn't take long however, to realise that being bubbly and eager to learn would only get me so far. The spirit of adventure quickly wore thin in my new role. Don't get me wrong, the people were lovely – but the work? Not so much. I felt like a fish out of water. I had no finance background, no understanding of the complexities of spreadsheets, or the sacred stewardship of other people's savings. I was a square peg trying to fit into a very, very round hole, and it left me feeling completely useless.

Not wanting to prolong the agony, I decided to tackle it head-on. My CEO was a decent sort, and we agreed to delay any talk of ending my new career, hoping I might experience a Damascus moment and suddenly fall in love with spreadsheets and financial jargon. But during my lunchbreaks, I quietly set my mind to getting back to the drawing board. It was time to pimp myself out – *again*.

I had learnt a lot from my previous effort, with brazenness topping the list. I came to appreciate that the worst thing that could happen was a polite 'no'. And if I could take no for an answer, I wasn't going to die wondering.

Fuelled by newfound boldness, I discovered a new prospect – the CEO of a mining company. They had recently relocated their headquarters from Melbourne to Adelaide. Seizing the opportunity, I figured I'd make my move. So, I slid into his LinkedIn DMs and told him I was too good to let slip through the cracks. I confessed that I couldn't quite quantify my value proposition yet – let's be real, I was still working through that shit. But I was ready to roll up my sleeves, head out to one of his mines and do some work – for free.

I wasn't sure what would come of it – probably a polite 'thank you, but...' Instead, to my utter surprise, Roger replied within the hour. His message started with 'LOL...' which, frankly, left me a little unsettled. Which part of my message had he found funny? Was it the 'too good to let slip through the cracks' line? Or maybe my bold offer to work for free, as if I were some kind of business philanthropist? Whatever the reason, I couldn't decide if I should be proud of myself for eliciting such a response or worried that I'd inadvertently made myself look like a twat.

Despite the ambiguity, he agreed to meet me for coffee and after a bit of contemplation, he decided to send me on a plane to a remote location in the state's north, where I could reacquaint myself with 'the outback'. Now, I wasn't entirely sure what he meant by that, but it sounded like a one-way ticket to either a life-changing adventure or a reality TV survival show. Maybe both. I had visions of myself stepping off a dusty plane into the wild, trying to blend in with the rugged Australian landscape, where I'd either learn something profound about myself or be disembowelled by a huge kangaroo – which, I now know, is technically possible according to the internet. But I didn't care. At this point, anything had to be better than spreadsheets and financial jargon. And if nothing else, losing the upper portion of my bowels would result in the loss of a few unwelcome kilos – so, win-win, right?

When I landed in the outback, it was clear that my 'reacquainting' was about to take a rather abrupt turn. The whole place was vast, dusty, and as fly ridden as I'd imagined. I took it all in, slightly overwhelmed, but energised by the freedom of the unknown. The mine site loomed ahead, and I could feel a sense of adventure pulsing through me. My first instinct was to start asking questions. And I mean *lots* of questions.

I'm pretty sure I wasn't exactly a hit with the workers, as I began my interrogation the moment we left Adelaide. I had no shame – marching up and down the aisles of the tiny twin-engine plane at five in the morning, waking the poor souls who had just managed to fall asleep, all in the name of 'gathering intel'. My unrelenting curiosity was met with blank stares, stifled groans, and more than a few awkward glances, but it didn't stop me – I was on a mission to succeed.

Once on site, I wasted no time and kept up my inquisition, speaking to anyone I could corner. I asked about everything from safety procedures to how they felt about the company's leadership style. The information I gathered, both in those early hours and throughout the rest of the day, was invaluable. It gave me a rock-solid foundation to start thinking about how to improve the company's performance, with a greater focus on listening to its people. Plus, I got to show everyone that I wasn't an out-of-place, clueless city girl. No, I was a curious, problem-solving force of nature from Haverhill, and I was here to make a difference!

Back in Adelaide, I worked late into the night sifting through all the data, distilling it into a slick, one-page summary that would hypothetically smack the reader in the face so hard they'd shit teeth for a week.

My one-time audition came a week later with Roger. As I apprehensively slid the A3 sheet I'd created across the table to him, I knew this was my one and only shot.

His eyebrows climbed higher and higher as he read through the content. 'Wow,' he said, clearly impressed. 'I'm amazed you unearthed so much in just one day.'

'Thank you, Roger,' I replied, deadpan. 'When you factor in the flight times, it was only half a day. Now, can I have a job?'

Roger looked pained. He explained that the company was a lean organisation, with no roles that fit my skillset. I could feel the door closing before it had even fully opened. As I was leaving, I turned to look straight at him. 'Well, will you be my mentor, then?' I blurted out.

Roger froze. Clearly, I'd caught him off guard. He didn't know what to say as I stood in his doorway, essentially blocking his exit.

'I take it that's a yes then?' I grinned. 'Great, I'll see you for an hour each month,' I rhetorically offered.

Our monthly mentoring sessions commenced a couple of weeks later, and at every meeting, I played along with the whole mentoring cover – asking the obligatory, 'How would you handle scenario X or Y?' And, of course, I took every opportunity to badger him for a role. After several mentoring sessions, I decided to ditch the pretence and get real.

'Roger, I am losing the spring in my step, so I'm leaving my job,' I said. 'So... if you are interested, I'd really love to work for your organisation.'

He didn't say much, just nodded and agreed to meet the following month. Just like with Hank, I left his office with my shoulders slumped, thinking I'd blown it. But as I opened the door to leave, he called me back.

'Would you like to join our upcoming executive planning day?' he offered.

I had to restrain myself from breakdancing on the spot. Performing the caterpillar to be precise, as I was pretty sure I would have nailed it in that moment of elation.

Fast forward to the executive strategy day, at which I was allocated a slot in the agenda to present a topic to the leadership team. This time, I actually read the brief properly and nailed it. The presentation was polished, well-received, and within days, after some discussions with his team, Roger offered me a contract to head up the company's innovation strategy. But he didn't stop there, he also gave me a seat as the lone female on his executive leadership team. I stood seven-feet tall and cried happy tears.

It was everything I had hoped for – an environment where I could challenge the norm and be unapologetically myself.

Within a couple more weeks, Roger handed me responsibility for the corporate affairs portfolio. I was finally on the professional path I'd been craving, and Roger was the kind of boss who not only helped me fight off the self-doubt that still lingered, but also encouraged me to embrace the abstract, weird side of my thinking. He helped me recognise how my unconventional background could actually be an asset to a business. He often quoted Steve Jobs, talking about the madness of hiring smart people and then telling them what to do. Roger didn't realise it, but he became my third guardian angel, injecting much-needed enthusiasm back into my life.

Finishing my contract with this incredible company was agonising, but I realised I wasn't Superwoman. I needed to find balance. I wanted to be present for a loved one recently diagnosed with cancer, I needed to be a good partner to my long-suffering LNT, and I longed to be a fully engaged mother to Amy. I would miss the pace of full-time work terribly, but I knew, at that time, leaving was the right decision.

> *Success isn't about having the perfect path or knowing every step in advance. It's about having the balls to stumble, dust oneself off, and keep moving forward anyway. Reinvention is rarely linear, and often the most uncomfortable experiences lead us to the greatest personal transformation. As Albert Einstein famously said, 'The only mistake that truly matters is not learning from the ones we make.'*

27

Champagne with that G-String?

Job offers, reunions, and the sudden reappearance of old flames all collided at once, pulling me in every direction. Just when I thought life had settled into a peaceful rhythm, I found myself juggling more than I ever imagined, while carrying the heavy emotional baggage of returning to my hometown after decades away. And just as I thought I had it all under control, life threw me a curveball that would shatter everything I thought I knew...

I had barely settled into my chair, ready to dive into writing my memoirs in early January 2017, when an email landed in my inbox demanding my attention. It was an offer of a contract to complete a challenging project within the Australian Court Jurisdiction. Now, you'd think that after just making the decision to leave full-time work for the best company ever, I'd ignore this and dive into my long-awaited writing, right? Nope, my fuckwit brain stepped in with other plans. It fired off a series of urgent messages to my fingers, which, obediently sprang into action. Before I knew it, I was typing an 'I'm in' response.

Fast forward a few weeks. Another email arrived, this time from a membership organisation. The CEO, with all the flair of a top recruiter, mentioned he'd heard that I had some capacity and was a 'gun for hire'.

I was flattered, but I knew I must politely decline, due to my book and my already-packed schedule with family and the courts. But, as usual, my inability to say no – combined with my ego's undeniable love affair with the phrase 'gun for hire' – took over. And before I knew it, I had accidentally screamed, 'I'm in!'

So, with these two contracts in my lap, plus the hours I'd committed to the mining company I'd just left, I was now fully booked for six bloody days a week. Now, completely entangled in other people's work, my book would just have to wait.

A few days later, my world as a certifiable workaholic was pleasantly interrupted by a Facebook post inviting me to a thirtieth reunion of my school year in my hometown of Haverhill. Instantly, the party girl in me screamed, 'Yes! Go!' But the now responsible grown-up replied, 'Sorry! Too far to travel and too many deadlines to meet.'

Then, LNT, the ever-practical voice of reason, chimed in with some classic wisdom. 'Get going. We're dead an awful long time, and who knows when the opportunity will come around again?'

That was all it took. No more debating. I booked my return flight faster than you can say long overdue trip down memory lane. It was a whirlwind five-day tour of the UK, ticking off family visits first and culminating in the much-anticipated school reunion on the Saturday night.

I landed on a Tuesday morning, hit the ground running, and immediately caught up with my parents and James. In between all the catching up, I made a quick call to Timmy – yes, that Timmy, the one who had left me a sobbing wreck for what should have been my first official date with a boy, more than thirty years ago. We arranged a pre-reunion drink at a local pub. What could possibly go wrong?

With the reunion fast approaching, it was time for a little pre-game. I met up with two of my dearest girlfriends from my Oxford days when I was living in the city – definitely not impressing anyone with my academic brilliance but certainly holding my own in the pub scene. We decided to rendezvous in Cambridge, the other famous university town, since it was conveniently close to my school reunion event.

We'd booked ourselves into a luxury health spa retreat, figuring it was the perfect spot to reconnect and catch up on all the gossip.

'This is oh so p-o-s-h,' joked my friend Sue, slipping into a fluffy white cotton dressing gown and leading us down the meandering corridors to the sauna and mud bath area. We were greeted by a woman who looked like she'd just stepped out of a yoga retreat, oozing health and sophistication. She gave us the rundown of the spa's offerings, before asking if we'd like a drink. I nodded eagerly, anticipating something fancy – preferably with a little umbrella in it...

'You'll be pleased to know we offer every herbal tea known to humankind,' she announced, 'and water.'

'Hmmm,' pondered Sue, hiding any disappointment, 'I reckon I'll go for the chamomile.'

'Make mine a mineral water, please,' said Jess, trying to sound as Zen as possible.

It was all just a bit too much for me. 'Do you have any Coke?' I asked, earning a look from her that could curdle milk. 'I'm sorry, but I just need some sugar,' I added quickly, trying to assure her I wasn't taking the piss and trying to ruin the spa vibe – I was just a genuine sugar addict who was lost in this unfamiliar world of wellness.

She gave me an almost pitying look but agreed to check what she could do. As she turned to leave, my two health-conscious friends – who'd been trying their best to pretend they were born with cucumber water running through their veins – couldn't resist.

'Well, if that's the case, can I have one too, please?' they chimed in unison.

Sue and Jess had spent the last half hour pretending to be high society, but deep down, they were still the same feral souls I knew and loved. Proof that while you might take the girl out of the council estate, there's fuck-all chance you can take the council estate out of the girl.

The instant sugar hit from our Cokes was like a bolt of lightning, and we were transformed into a bunch of gossiping schoolgirls, sharing stories and shrieking with ever-greater moments of tummy-grabbing laughter. Clearly, the raucous laughter was not what is expected at such a salubrious establishment. A very stiff-lipped staff member poked her head in to see what the ruckus was about.

'Ladies,' she said, her tone colder than a polar vortex, 'we do have other clients who are trying to relax. If you would keep the noise down, please?'

Suitably chastised, we tried to behave like adults.

Being an adult lasted about five minutes before we headed to the much-anticipated mud bath, where we could wrestle, and fling it at each other like the children we were at heart. Disappointment doesn't even begin to describe how I felt when I saw a pretty little dish, the sort you would place dipping sauce in, topped up with rust-coloured clay.

'All very civilised,' I said with an air of fake refinement, scooping out a dollop and applying it to my face like I was some kind of spa goddess.

'Civilised it might be,' Jess muttered, eyeing the clay like it was a cruel joke, 'but how the hell is this tiny amount supposed to cover my arse, let alone my whole body?'

After the mud bath letdown, we were ushered into separate rooms for the highlight of the day – the body wrap. A sharply dressed therapist greeted me with a polite smile and pointed to a table, which, much to my confusion, held a couple of packets of disposable underwear. I tore open the first packet and found a G-string that looked more like a face mask. I slipped the scanty item on then opened the other packet. I was flummoxed to find... another G-string! I held it up, turned it this way and that, and after much contemplation, I transformed it into what I hoped would pass as a makeshift bra – a very makeshift bra that was doing absolutely no favours for my expensive but worth-it ample bangers. I tugged it into place, wrapped a modesty towel around myself, and braced for the therapy session.

When the therapist returned, she barely contained a giggle as she surveyed my 'disposable bikini', her face a portrait of pity.

'Um, madam,' she said, biting her lip, 'we supply two sets of G-strings in case our larger clients break one.'

I tried to play it cool, despite the lingering suggestion that I might still be a fat c.u.n.t. 'Oh, I didn't break one,' I said, trying to salvage a shred of dignity, 'so I thought I'd get inventive with the spare one...'

The next morning, I emerged from the health spa feeling oddly elated. As I drove to the town of my youth, I felt a sense of pride. Sure, I'd been a spa disaster, but at least I hadn't broken one of the G-strings!

I slowed down as I approached Haverhill, savouring the moment. I knew what I was heading into – no mud bath surprises here. It felt like a warm, comforting certainty. First stop, the local fish and chip shop for a saveloy and chips with lashings of vinegar. As I walked down the high street, memories of my wild youth flooded back. I stopped by the pub where I'd spent many fun nights. Now it was boarded up and looking like a perfect spot for a developer, or squatter to snap up – whichever came first.

Next, I made my way to the first home I bought for James and me to live in. A place where we had laughed, cried and sought sanctuary. A little further down was the park where I'd spent many single-mum afternoons with James, pushing him on the swings to while the time away. Not much had changed – except for the dog poo bin, which had mysteriously disappeared. But, in true Haverhill fashion, the locals diligently left their dogs' crap in little bags on the ground where the bin once stood. It was oddly heartwarming to observe.

My stroll ended at the railway track, where I'm pretty sure James was conceived. I paused, taking in the gravity of the moment. Thirty years ago, destiny had intervened...

As I made my way back to the car, I felt a strange mix of nostalgia and pride. My former life in Haverhill felt far removed from the one I was living now, but it had shaped everything. It felt good. It would always be home.

The poignancy of the moment was matched only by what followed – a drink at the local pub with the boy who'd broken my heart. Yes, Timmy – my first love, who had stood me up on our first date when I was just eleven. The guy who left me love-sick and grief-stricken to the point where my dad stormed over to his house to tell his mother what a dreadful son she had.

I had reached out to him on Facebook, and we agreed to meet at the local pub before the reunion. He seemed genuinely keen – though given his track record, I half-expected to be stood up again. But there he was, standing at the bar, thirty-five years later. And even after all those years, my heart skipped a beat as I gave him a hug. It felt like unfinished business.

He offered to buy me a drink, and I asked for a glass of bubbly. 'I'll have a bottle of Moët,' Timmy said, gesturing to the bartender.

What? Was he trying to make up for the years of heartbreak with a bottle of champagne? Was this the Timmy Apology Tour, priced at about a pound a year for every tear shed? It seemed like the perfect moment to bring up the suffering of my eleven-year-old self... 'Timmy, you broke my heart that day,' I announced as he poured champagne into my glass.

'I didn't mean to,' he replied, looking truly sincere.

'But you did, Timmy,' I pressed. 'You broke my heart. You know that right?'

'Yes,' he said, 'but I've wanted to explain myself ever since.'

'Well, now's your chance,' I said gulping a big swig of bubbly, intrigued by what was about to come.

He took a deep breath. 'When I showed up at your house, the music was so loud I couldn't hear a thing. I knocked on the door over and over, but all I could hear was *Stop, Wait a Minute Mr Postman*. I honestly thought you were taking the piss out of me.'

'Bullshit, Timmy,' I said, laughing.

'I swear! I knocked on your door for ages, eventually thinking that you had intentionally turned your music up because you didn't want to see me.'

I stared at him in disbelief. 'Are you serious?'

'Deadly serious. I have no reason to lie. I eventually gave up knocking and walked away, gutted. I was too embarrassed to arrive at the party alone, so I went by the local youth club and asked a random girl if she would come to the disco with me. Next thing I know, my mum storms in, grabs me by the scruff of the neck, and drags me home. She told me I needed to apologise to your dad, or I'd never have a chance with you. Terrified of your dad, I did just that.'

I was stunned into silence. When I finally found my voice, I said, 'I had no idea. Timmy, this is the first time I've heard that version of events.'

'Well,' he said, looking sheepish, 'I did try to tell you. I saw you in a pub a few years later and when I approached you, you told me to get fucked.'

That sounded plausible. I was probably all wrapped up in some other guy by then.

'And you know, I felt the same way about you. But then you met Max and had a baby together, and that put an end to everything.'

Somehow, hearing that gave me the closure I needed. He hadn't meant to break my heart. We were two children who failed to communicate with each other properly, which it seems followed us both into our adult lives.

It was time to say goodbye, not knowing if our lives would ever cross again. We shared a tearful hug before he disappeared into the crowd, and I made my way to the taxi that would take me to my school reunion.

If you believe that school days are the best days of your life, then a thirty-year reunion is like stepping out of a time machine that takes you right back to those days. Walking into that room, it felt as if no time had passed at all. Despite the years, the wrinkles, and the life stories, it was clear that we were still the same people we had been. We had all stayed true to ourselves.

Out of the hundred or so students from our year, around seventy showed up – a pretty good turnout, considering some lived overseas, some were untraceable, and too many had passed away.

Partners weren't invited – just the old classmates. The familiar banter from years gone by returned quickly, and in most cases, the girls recognised each other right away. We all looked like slightly worn-out versions of our younger selves. The boys, on the other hand, were a challenge. Most of them had been weedy, acne-covered lads with no facial hair the last time I'd seen them. Now, they were men – some bearded, some balding, and all a bit rounder. Thank God for the name tags that I would surreptitiously glance down at before offering a hug.

Among the group of us were three couples who had stayed together since they were about eleven. Watching them dance together, still content in each other's company, was beautiful. I found myself in total awe of them – hell, I was in awe of everyone in that room.

My teenage nemesis was there – the girl Max had been in an on-again, off-again relationship with throughout our school years. But we were no longer rivals. We were adults now, life had softened our edges, and we'd both come through relatively unscathed, without the scars of our youth defining us.

The reunion turned out to be therapeutic in ways I didn't expect, helping me close a chapter and realise just how far I'd come. If I'd stayed in Haverhill, I genuinely don't think I'd still be alive. My mother had been right – I was a 'silly, silly girl' back then.

As I left the reunion that night, a woman I've known since I was four held me tightly. 'This is probably the last time I'm ever going to see you, isn't it?' she said while looking deeply into my eyes. The words hit me harder than I expected. She was probably right. My life was in Australia now, and that was now where I truly belonged.

As I flew back to Australia, a sense of peace settled within me. Life, it seemed, was finally starting to make sense.

Just when I thought I had everything figured out, the rug was yanked out from under me. We were sitting on the sofa, the hum of our quiet home around us, when LNT turned to me with an unsettling coldness in his eyes and said, 'I'm leaving you.'

Life, they say, is fleeting. And yet here I was, stuck in a loop of rinse-and-repeat. Through it all, we hold the power to heal and continue moving forward...

Erm... fuck that wisdom bollocks!

Acknowledgements

A huge shoutout to my long-suffering friends who pushed, prodded, and sometimes kicked me in the right direction so I could grow a pair of balls big enough to release this book.

Son, we've been through it all together. Your patience with my shitty life choices is truly infinite. You make me proud every day.

Daughter, you are awesome. And a note to your future spouse: this one shines brightly, try to dim that light and I'll hunt you down.

Mum and Dad, now I have a teenage daughter, I finally get it. Sorry for swearing, experimenting with drugs, and having sex with more than three people. At least you didn't have a vanilla daughter – even if sometimes it would have been preferred. I love you both.

Bro, I owe you big time. Thanks for enduring a lifetime of listening to my shit.

My life-changing bosses, you taught me that embracing difference is a superpower. Thanks for setting me free, and for not firing me.

To my readers, past, present and future. **This book is for you.**

www.ingramcontent.com/pod-product-compliance
Ingram Content Group UK Ltd.
Pitfield, Milton Keynes, MK11 3LW, UK
UKHW030823310325
5233UKWH00027B/125